6 SECRETS FOR DELIVERING IMPOSSIBLE PROJECTS

6 SECRETS

FOR

DELIVERING IMPOSSIBLE PROJECTS

A Practical Guide for Conquering Your Company's Hardest Challenges

Mark G. Cooper, PhD

CONFLUENT CRESCENT

ISBN: 979-8-9915400-0-1

Library of Congress Control Number: 2024919139

First Paperback Edition September 2024
10 9 8 7 6 5 4 3 2 1

Printed in the United States of America by IngramSpark

Cover Design by Emily Whiting

Published by Confluent Crescent, Cordova, Tennessee
Visit www.confluentcrescent.com

Dedicated to partners and friends who participated in Impossible Projects with me, including Lamora, Mike, Tim, Laura, Kassaundra, Govan, Allison, Rajesh, Walt, Donna, Tamala, Lisa, Bill, Julie, Al, Scott, Tom, Cheryl, and KSB.

Contents

Introduction

The auditorium was beginning to fill when I arrived. Alongside me were the two people with whom I had worked most closely for the past eighteen months. We sat together toward the front. For the next several minutes, a steady stream of people entered and took their seats. Groups assembled and joined via video conference at other locations as well.

That day we all gathered to celebrate the delivery of the largest single-load project in the company's history. It implemented fundamental changes to customer capabilities, business processes, operational procedures, and data pathways.

The project touched more than one hundred different applications, and I had led a team of more than forty architects and subject matter experts. I turned and looked at the crowd behind me. It was amazing and gratifying and humbling to see everyone in the auditorium, and to stand atop that pyramid.

Two years earlier, the smart money said that there was no way that the project could be accomplished, but the team came through. Doubt lingered even as late as a few weeks before the target date, but the soft launch went so well that the product was released to the broader market several months earlier than planned. We had delivered an Impossible Project.

—

Most of the time we do Ordinary Projects. Some are harder than others. Some are more or less interesting. Some are more or less impactful. But most are necessary. They keep the company running. They keep product moving and revenue flowing. They facilitate continuous incremental improvement.

Unfortunately, we will occasionally end up on a Death March. As the name suggests they are uninspiring, unnecessarily difficult, sometimes unnecessary altogether, and always draining. Some of the project objectives might be delivered, but a trail of wreckage is left behind. The First Secret will show you how to recognize a Death March so that you can avoid it if possible.

But once in a while, a project comes along that is palpably different. You will recognize it when you see it. A project that has the potential to drive substantive change or deliver a breakthrough innovation. You know that it will be challenging. Maybe it's been tried unsuccessfully before. Maybe people are lined up down the hall ready to tell you that it can't be done. But if there's a customer, clarity of vision, and management support, you can deliver it. It's not just an Ordinary Project. It's an Impossible Project.

I love Impossible Projects.

I would actively pursue these projects, and I've had the opportunity to work on several during my career. In some cases the project was overwhelmingly large and complex. In others, the prerequisite technology didn't exist. Once I was laughed at for suggesting what I thought was a reasonable solution. In each instance, and against the prevailing wisdom, we successfully delivered.

—

This book will be most useful for those whom psychologists describe as having a *clutch mentality*. The basketball player who calls for the ball to make the last-second shot. The singer who gives her best performances in the limelight at center stage. The paramedic who is always first on the scene caring for the most seriously injured. The executive whose calm decisiveness secures the deal despite challenging negotiations.

And the leader who seeks out and delivers Impossible Projects.

Sometimes the scenarios are more mundane, but they're no less indicative. Maybe you look forward to completing the *New York Times* crossword puzzle each Sunday. Maybe you're not a very good artist but still prefer the Difficult category in *Pictionary*. Maybe you start with Potpourri for $1000 please, Alex. Maybe you just like solving hard problems.

If any of these scenarios sound familiar, then this book is for you.

My goal is to help you to identify extraordinary projects, Impossible Projects, so that you can pursue them, lead them, and succeed with them. It is practical advice born of experience.

Although the Secrets revealed in this book are useful for management, the intended audience are non-management business and technical leaders, as well as those who aspire to leadership. You may, though, discover that the advice shared here applies to any role in any project. Be the leader of your own domain, even if you're just starting out and your domain has a population of one.

I do not presuppose that you have any direct reports. Instead, the focus is on indirect influence. It's about motivating, inspiring, and leading by example. It's about nurturing relationships, being open to feedback, and recognizing that in the best case most everyone else on your team will know more about their domains than you do. In fact, if you discover that you know more than anyone else on your project team, the subject matter expert role (SME) might be more appropriate for you than the lead role. I'll talk about that more with the Fourth Secret.

Leading an Impossible Project is also a balancing act. You must articulate the broad vision while orchestrating the steps required to accomplish it. You must inspire your team with that vision while keeping them focused on the task at hand. You must see *what could be* at the same time as *what is* without conflating the two. You must earn the trust of your three constituencies–team, management, customers–and demand honesty and forthrightness from them.

—

I didn't start out intending to develop a methodology for delivering Impossible Projects, and I never went into any of these projects with a specific plan or formula. Rather, these

Secrets evolved over time as they were successful on one project and applied to the next.

The Six Secrets are presented in roughly the order you would expect to apply them during a project, starting before you are even officially on board and extending through its delivery.

Finally, although these thoughts, ideas, and opinions are seasoned with experience, they may not all work for you. There is no cookbook or algorithm for leadership. You must ultimately find your own way, but my hope is that these Secrets will give you the tools to identify and successfully deliver your Impossible Projects.

Mark G. Cooper
September 9, 2024

First Secret

Recognize the Difference Between an Impossible Project and a Death March

An email addressed to the project team arrived shortly after lunch announcing the launch of the new business system. It was effusive in its praise of the team, and optimistic about the project's benefits to the company. Most recipients briefly scanned it, filed it, and largely ignored it.

A celebratory conference call was scheduled for the following day where a couple of executives popped on for a minute to tell everyone what a great job they had done, before dropping off for other meetings. That was OK, though, because only a small fraction of the team attended.

For the past year, nobody had been immune to the seemingly unceasing tongue-lashings from both their own management as well as from their customer's. Mentioning the constantly changing requirements, frequent staff turnover, and unrealistic deadlines was seen as making excuses and brought forth more wrath. Furthermore, corporate standards mandated a platform that was not built for that kind of application. It was a miracle, and testament to the talent and perseverance of the project team, that anything functional was delivered at all.

But now everyone was weary. The project felt wet and filthy and clingy, like clothing after trudging across a muddy field in a rainstorm. And all anybody wanted was to get it off and throw it into the corner. Those that survived this Death March to the end had quickly moved on to other projects.

———

The most reliable way to differentiate an Impossible Project from a Death March is to observe the team's morale when the project is finished. At the end of an Impossible Project the team will be exhausted, certainly, but also energized, their drive and creativity invigorated. They embraced the vision and goal of the project. They believed that they had a chance to do something significant, and they succeeded against the odds. They are excited and proud to see the product being used, and ready to take on the next challenge.

At the end of a Death March, the team will also be exhausted. Just exhausted. And probably demoralized and defeated. They made it to the end, but only because the boats had been burned at the shore and there wasn't another choice. Maybe they can point to something that they're proud to have delivered. Every cloud has a silver lining, they say, but nobody's very happy. Everyone just wants to put the whole sorry episode behind them. I've seen entire teams dissolve and scatter at the end of one of these projects.

Of course, having to wait until the end of the project to discover which kind you have isn't very helpful. You really need to know at the outset, and even before. That way you can identify and pursue projects that, while difficult, will be rewarding and avoid those that will suck the life out of you and your team.

Death Marches

Edward Yourdon wrote the book* on Death Marches. Literally. He defines a Death March as a project where one or more "'project parameters' exceed the norm by at least 50 percent." Those parameters include schedule, staff, budget, and requirements or other technical aspects. So, you've got a Death March if the schedule is too tight by half, or you have too few people by half, or too little funding by half, and so forth.

He also characterizes it as a project "for which an unbiased, objective risk assessment determines that the likelihood of failure is ≥ 50%."

His book has a ton of great advice about how to deal with a Death March project. You can do a lot to turn one around, and the project may succeed, perhaps even with a minimum of destruction left in its wake.

My purpose is to not replicate that advice here. In fact, I'm going to deviate from his definition shortly, but if you're considering leading an Impossible Project, it would be worthwhile to read Yourdon's book. Go ahead, I'll wait.

OK. Here's where I differ:

> **Death Marches of the kind described by Yourdon are unnecessary. They are the result of a misalignment of schedule, staff, budget, and/or scope that could be resolved if there was the will to do it. They are the result of poor management and/or poor leadership.**

---

*Yourdon, Edward. *Death March (Second Edition)*. Upper Saddle River, NJ: Pearson Education, Inc., 2004.

Subjecting a team to artificial challenges is a huge red flag, and is not characteristic of management and/or leadership with whom you are likely to be successful. More often than not, this behavior reflects management focusing solely on itself and not on the team, the customer, or the product.

Sometimes the assignment of a Death March is used by management as a weapon or a test. Keeping a subordinate rival occupied with an impossible task dates back beyond antiquity. Just ask Uriah, who was sent into battle by King David and was ultimately killed so that the king could have Uriah's wife Bathsheba for himself.

As for a test, everyone knows when something is being made unnecessarily difficult. Maybe the team will be on board if they understand that success in this project will lead to something more substantial, but again this is unnecessary. There are better ways to evaluate one's mettle without wasting time with contrived challenges.

Instead of the percentages used by Yourdon, my definitions for Impossible Project and Death March are based on certain project characteristics. Assuming that the benefit identified for both types of projects is sufficiently high to justify pursuing them:

An Impossible Project has high intrinsic difficulty.

A Death March has unnecessarily high extrinsic difficulty.

Let's look at these definitions more closely.

Intrinsic and Extrinsic Difficulty

We want to evaluate the "difficulty" of a project, but the term itself is so broad as to not be very useful. For our purposes, the key dimension of difficulty is its source: either intrinsic or extrinsic. Understanding this difference is essential to differentiating an Impossible Project from a Death March.

Intrinsic Difficulty describes challenges inherent to the project or problem itself. The solution may be complex, necessitating the coordination of many different components. It may be complicated, demanding the application of techniques or technologies which may not exist...yet. It may challenge long-held assumptions or transform entrenched business processes. The key, though, is that the team can resolve intrinsic challenges through its own effort, dedication, and creativity. The Fifth Secret addresses the importance of recognizing and resolving the most important intrinsic challenges.

Extrinsic Difficulty describes challenges imposed by outside forces that the team generally cannot directly affect. A substantial portion of your effort as lead will be spent mitigating extrinsic challenges.

The intrinsic difficulty of a problem or project dictates its minimum extrinsic requirements. A project will necessarily require some minimum time and resources simply by the nature of what needs to be accomplished. The goal of management is to find that minimum, and then squeeze just a little more. Of course, the project may devolve into a Death March if squeezed too much.

Examples of Extrinsic Factors

From Yourdon's Death March Definition	Schedule
	Staff
	Budget
	Scope
Non-Functional Requirements	Performance
	Reliability
	Scalability
	Availability
Corporate Standards	Project Management Methodology
	Application Instrumentation
	Pre-Selected Hardware / Software
	Data Management Requirements
	Information Security Requirements
Human Factors	Organizational Structure
	Interpersonal Dynamics
	Customer Demand
	Corporate Culture

Conversely, certain extrinsic factors, especially non-functional requirements, can create intrinsic challenges. For example, strict user performance expectations may necessitate the implementation of a novel methodology, when more relaxed requirements could have been accommodated using a simpler approach.

Some leaders, perhaps those with a spreadsheet management orientation, gravitate toward projects where the focus is on the extrinsic constraints. They relish the challenge of delivering a solution with meager funding in as little time and with as few people as possible. Their focus is on *how* the project is accomplished. When successful, that approach can be beneficial for them and for their own career advancement, but really they are looking to be heroes on the backs of their team. The probability of a Death March is very high, and I would recommend avoiding these folks altogether.

Other leaders, perhaps those with an engineering orientation, find projects with intrinsic challenges more interesting and rewarding to solve. Their focus is on *what* the project accomplishes. They look for opportunities that will inspire their team and problems that will stimulate innovation and creativity.

Net Benefit

The second dimension we'll look at when differentiating Impossible Projects from Death Marches is benefit. Every project is expected to return some value for the company, but like difficulty, "benefit" has innumerable meanings. Here we'll just consider it in the abstract aggregate. Your project could drive increased sales, decreased cost, new customers, promotional campaign lift, operational efficiency, or any number of other advantages. The beneficiaries are equally diverse: external customers, employees, suppliers, shareholders, etc. Obviously we all want to work on projects that provide substantial benefit.

But it's not enough to focus on the benefits alone. Cost must be included in the equation.

Generally speaking, the costs associated with the intrinsic difficulty of a new project are considered when it is first analyzed for prioritization. Estimating the cost to deliver is a fundamental management skill. What are the required roles and how many team members are needed for each? How many consultants and contractors? How much training? How much time? How much hardware and software? And so on.

For your purposes, you must go one step further and examine the costs associated with the known and potential extrinsic challenges. They are difficult to quantify and fortunately you don't have to. It is enough that you recognize them and understand the magnitude of the impact that they may have on the project. We'll talk more about assessing difficulty later in this chapter, but a project's monetary benefit can be more than negated by its extrinsic costs.

Therefore, when categorizing projects, it's better to evaluate "net benefit," taking into account both the intrinsic and extrinsic difficulty costs.

Project Categorization

With a foundational understanding of intrinsic and extrinsic difficulty, as well as of net benefit, we can now describe four project types as graph quadrants.

High	Death March	Impossible Project
Intrinsic Difficulty	Ordinary Project	Low-Hanging Fruit
Low		
	Low Net Benefit	**High**

Project Category Quadrants

Since Impossible Projects and Death Marches are the focus of this chapter, let's look briefly at the other two.

Low-Hanging Fruit are to many the most attractive corporate projects. Nearly every project management book advises leaders to find "quick wins" to build credibility and momentum. This is certainly a good approach, but at some point you will discover that all of the Low-Hanging Fruit has been picked and that doing anything consequential requires more effort. This is especially true with mature organizations and products that have been examined by talented teams many times before.

Ordinary Projects keep the corporate wheels turning and drive continuous improvement. They can be used to gain experience as well as to build credibility and momentum. Your company probably has hundreds, maybe thousands in progress at any given time.

Rethinking our diagram quadrants, Ordinary Projects actually consume much, much more than a quarter of the grid, which probably shouldn't be divided into quadrants. Rather, the other three categories live at the corners, and Ordinary Projects consume all of the remaining space. Furthermore, the boundaries between categories are fuzzy and overlapping, not crisp.

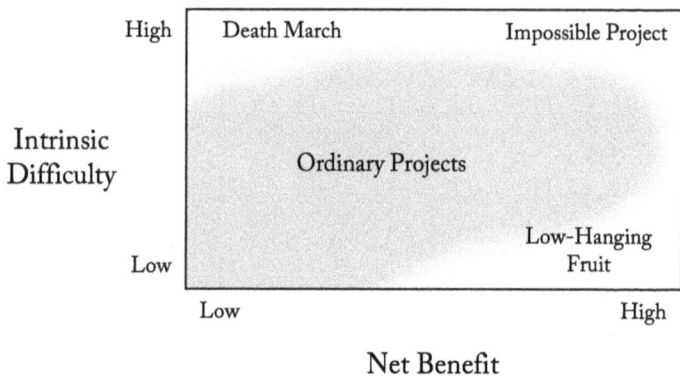

A More Realistic Depiction of Project Categories

Assessing Benefit

This is usually the easy part. By the time you hear about the existence of a project, its value has almost certainly already been established. In addition to financial or business benefit,

Impossible Projects exhibit one or more of the following:

The objective has never been accomplished, or was previously unsuccessfully attempted.

The objective transforms culture, technology, and/or business process.

The objective challenges long-held assumptions and paradigms.

The objective requires complex interactions between systems and capabilities, and may even require the creation of new ones.

The objective necessitates the involvement of many disparate teams.

An Impossible Project requires creativity and problem solving, and provides opportunities for learning and development. Sometimes this takes the form of structured training. Sometimes it is simply the exposure to team members from other parts of the company whose collective knowledge, experience, and expertise are required to overcome the barriers that had previously made the project impossible.

An Impossible Project, to borrow from Steve Jobs, makes a dent in the universe. You and your team can make a meaningful impact, and the satisfaction that brings cannot be quantified on a balance sheet.

Trust your intuition and your instincts. You know your company. You know its processes, culture, and conventional wisdom. You know your customers' demands. And you know where the potential lies for consequential change.

Assessing Difficulty

This part is much harder. This is really where you determine whether it's more likely that you're looking at an Impossible Project or at a Death March. This is where you will decide whether or not you want to have anything to do with the project. And even if you've been assigned and don't have a choice, assess it anyway so that you can try to take appropriate corrective action if necessary.

The three factors to consider most carefully are: customer demand, customer clarity, and management support.

Customer Demand

Start by identifying those who will be impacted by the project, both inside and outside your company. What is the magnitude of that impact, and is it positive or negative? Are you adding useful capabilities or are you taking them away? Perhaps adoption will require a learning curve and that's to be expected, but in the end, does it improve their job, process, workflow, or life? Is your project doing something *for* them, or is it doing something *to* them?

After all, if you aren't focused on "wowing" your customer, then what is going to motivate you and/or your team when faced with setbacks? What kind of support will you get from your customer? Demand is crucial from the beginning and throughout the project.

Be honest and objective.

Obviously, you want your project to benefit those who will use its deliverables, providing new capabilities or improving existing ones. Even better if the users requested them, and even better still if they are excited about or eagerly anticipating them. It generates enthusiasm about the project that can carry you, your team, your management, and your company.

Sometimes an Impossible Project is required to create marketplace demand. Post-It notes and VCRs come to mind. The "build it and they will come" approach. This can be risky for those green-lighting the project, but being first-to-market can pay huge dividends when customers are given something they didn't know they could have or didn't know they needed.

But beware when you see that demand, benefit, and impact are not aligned. One constituency may want the project to happen and expects to enjoy the benefits from it, while another is negatively impacted. Such a misalignment is particularly worrisome when it's the users that are on the short end of it. This is a very early, very reliable sign of an impending Death March. At best, the users will be grudgingly compliant. At worst, they will be intransigent or actively hostile. These projects often do not move the company forward despite consuming a tremendous amount of effort, and working hard on a project that the users don't want is demoralizing to yourself, your team, and the users themselves. Furthermore, the demand is likely artificial and the whole project may collapse under the weight of the push-back.

Customer Clarity

If you're like me, every so often you arrive home in the evening hungry, but having no idea what to make for supper. "What do you want to eat?" gets volleyed back and forth.

Customer demand alone is not enough. Neither is a vague description of the deliverables. Specificity and clarity are required. The customer experience should be fully described, even if the details about how it will all happen are not yet known.

Most companies that release products and services for external consumption have dedicated teams assigned to be the voice of the customer (VOC). They survey and interview customers, and digest their feedback, advice, and suggestions. The customer, or their proxy, should be involved throughout the project. They are best able to articulate the vision and objectives. When we get to the Third Secret, we'll see that these VOC teams often create stories of how different types of customers will interact with the project deliverables. These are great to see, and indicative of a team that is at least aspiring to clarity and probably accomplishing it.

In the Third Secret we'll also talk more about your role in achieving clarity of purpose. Suffice it to say that at this point you can't know everything, but it's critical that you recognize whether any uncertainty remains about who the customer is, how they will use your product, or why they want or need it. Don't ever try to sweep those questions under the rug, or hope that explanations will reveal themselves eventually. They probably won't.

Management Support

Customer demand and clarity can go a long way toward keeping a team engaged and optimistic, even in the face of the longest odds. This is what motivates the team to be creative and to think about solutions, even on their own time. Teams have an incredible capacity for extraordinary feats. Team members will remain with an Impossible Project long after they would have abandoned a Death March. But all of that can be irreparably compromised if you don't have the appropriate management support.

Management must fundamentally decide whether they really want the project to be delivered, and they must decide how easy or difficult they want to make it for the project team. You might wonder whether we really need to go there. Absolutely! The team will require resources and prioritization. Challenges and setbacks are inevitable. Obstacles and roadblocks will require clearing. The team will need air cover, diplomacy, and border defenses. Just as the team needs to buy into the vision of the project, management must as well. Extrinsic difficulties are almost always the consequence of management choices.

It's trite but true: management support is a critical success factor, especially for an Impossible Project. "Management support," however, has become this amorphous blank-slate concept that can mean anything to anybody, inevitably leading to misunderstandings and miscommunication. Let's see if we can be more concrete.

In short, you are looking for management to help with the extrinsic challenges, especially resources, prioritization, accountability, advocacy, and schedule.

Resources: This one probably goes without saying, but we'll talk a little bit about it anyway. It most commonly refers to funding and personnel, but also includes supplies, raw materials, technology, data, and physical space.

Resource projections are made long before implementation details are known, and the estimates are almost always conservative. That's just the way budgeting works. As a result, you can be confident that you won't have all of the resources you want.

But just as management makes its best guess about required resources, you will need to make your best guess as well. You won't have all of the implementation details either, but as you learn more about the project you will start to get an idea of what it will take to accomplish it. In the best case, the guesses will be close to each other, but ultimately the goal is to secure enough resources to give you and your team a reasonable chance of success.

At some point you will need to quantify and communicate the need for more resources as well as the consequences of not getting them. When that happens, think about your answer from the perspective of the question, "What will it take to produce the deliverable?" It's OK to not get two more developers added to the team as long as it's also OK to take three extra weeks to deliver. We'll discuss those kinds of trade-offs with the Second Secret.

Don't expect to always be successful. Project teams complain about resources so frequently that management becomes numb to these requests, often ignoring or denying them out of hand.

Questions you should ask include:

How much funding has been allocated for the project?

How many employees, contractors, and consultants are expected to participate in the project?

Are other resources like supplies, raw materials, physical space, and hardware and software expected to be needed? Have they been allocated or included in the budget?

Are your estimates close to management's estimates?

Prioritization: One characteristic of Death March projects, as defined by Yourdon, is that they are understaffed by at least fifty percent. That only tells half the story. Having the right people with the right skills is at least as important as having the right number of people.

Early in the project you will probably start doing background work in areas with which you're not familiar. This requires you to engage subject matter experts (SMEs) from those other areas. You know the best analysts, architects, developers, and project managers at your company. So, too, does management. These SMEs are always in high demand. Your management will need to advocate for your project, pushing to prioritize their participation. The right SMEs' availability for your project is one of the earliest and clearest indicators of management support, as well as where your project sits on the priority list.

As the project progresses, work with management to ensure that its priority does not decrease. It's easy for them to be excited about your shiny new initiative, only to redirect their SMEs toward the next shiny new initiative before they have finished yours. Of course, you may not know until it's too late, so pay particular attention.

Questions you should ask include:

How difficult is it to get assistance from the SMEs you need?

How much of their time will you get? Is that sufficient?

How responsive is their management to requests for their participation?

Is management committed to seeing the project through without redirecting resources when the next thing comes along?

How much political capital, if any, is your management willing to spend to get those SMEs on your project?

Accountability: Each individual on an Impossible Project takes ownership of their actions, decisions, and outcomes. Such a culture of accountability starts with executive management and permeates all of leadership. There is not the time, energy, or resources for anything less.

Roles, responsibilities, and expectations are clearly articulated, along with the metrics used to monitor and measure progress. Everyone understands what is expected of them. We'll talk more about this in the Third Secret.

When things go wrong, and they will, focus on solving the problem rather than on assigning blame. Learn from mistakes, then move on. These episodes can be motivating when handled properly.

I once messed up a piece of a project and got called into the Vice President's office. I was not looking forward to that meeting. When I arrived, there was no doubt that he was unhappy. After a few minutes, though, the conversation turned toward fixing the mistake. We explored several options. A half-hour later I left energized and inspired.

Accountability must be accompanied by empowerment, with you and your team making decisions within your areas of expertise without management being elbows-deep into the details. Of course, this applies to you, too. After all, you are relying on your SMEs for their expertise.

Finally, acknowledge your team's milestones, insightful ideas, and difficult problems solved. Management can provide funding for awards and celebrations. Be sure to budget for these, even if it's only a small amount.

Questions you should ask include:

> How experienced are the managers in their own domains? Do they try to dictate solutions? Do they micro-manage?

> How clearly can management articulate roles,

responsibilities, expectations, and metrics?

Has management handled past project difficulties constructively or destructively?

Have funds been allocated in the project budget for recognition and celebrations?

Advocacy: A friend applied for a Vice President position. During his interview with the Senior VP, he was asked the question, "What is the primary job of a Vice President?" He answered with the usual responsibilities including setting direction, articulating a vision, organizing staff, and managing the budget. The Senior VP replied that while those are all important, the primary job of a Vice President is sales. As a Vice President, he would need to persuade his peers to support his initiatives and priorities.

This doesn't just apply to Vice Presidents, but to all leadership, including you. Projects compete for limited time and resources, especially from core groups whose participation is required in most projects. The SMEs that you need may also be needed by other projects. Everybody involved in the project from the executive sponsor to the summer intern should always be advocating for it. Excitement is contagious.

One of the cliches frequently used to describe management support is "clearing the path." In addition to securing resources, this includes arbitrating disputes and resolving conflicts. At some point, something unexpected will happen. Maybe it has become clear that the team is going to miss a critical date. Perhaps an overlooked prerequisite capability must be built. Sometimes an exception to a standard process will be required. It could be anything. You are going to need management to smooth it over with other teams and customers, as well as with upper management. The better the relationship between management in the participating areas, the less severe of a problem these eventualities will create for you, your team, and your project.

Questions you should ask include:

> How open is management to negotiating and working with other areas?

> How assertively are they already advocating for the project?

> Is there any friction between teams participating in the project, especially among management?

Schedule: Nobody likes deadlines but everybody recognizes that they are necessary. The project usually comes with an overall target delivery date. Maybe it's the next regular product release, or maybe it's a featured demonstration at the annual trade show or conference. Maybe it's a race against the competition.

Your project may also be a dependency for activities that are beyond your scope or visibility. Product launches must be carefully timed, with advertising and media purchased several months ahead of time. Training may need to be created and delivered.

Sometimes, though, these deadlines are artificial. And political. Promises are made. Favors are exchanged. In order to avoid embarrassment, meeting that date becomes the most important thing in the world. Yet, in a year, no, in a couple of months, nobody is going to care.

The liability of turning the project into a Death March is much greater than the benefit of delivering on an artificial timeline.

The point is that some unmovable dates are more unmovable than others. We'll talk more about time and scope trade-offs with the Second Secret.

While you may not have any control over the ultimate delivery date, you will have control over the intermediate milestones. You may discover that there simply is not enough time to complete all of the milestones before the delivery date. It is your obligation to escalate that concern the moment you recognize it. You also need to have a recommendation for what it will take to deliver on time.

My preference is to propose to my team delivery dates that are unrealistically aggressive. In the best case, I guessed wrong and they are reasonable after all, but that never happens. The responses more typically range from disbelief to borderline rebellion. So, I ask the team for more reasonable dates. More often than not their dates are acceptable so we go with them and I hold the team to them. And they almost always deliver on their timeframes. Listen to your people. They know best.

Questions you should ask include:

> What is driving the ultimate delivery date?
>
> Does it look like the final delivery date is feasible or unreasonable?
>
> How flexible is the delivery date?
>
> What are the consequences of delay?
>
> What intermediate deliverables are expected and when?

—

Two comments before wrapping up this section. First, it is often useful to have a "contract," usually an email, outlining what management will provide, what the team will provide, and how success will be incrementally measured along the way. Even if it seems unnecessary or if management is reluctant to put something like this in writing, expectations should nevertheless be incorporated into the project documentation and communicated.

Second, it is unreasonable for you or your team to expect management to give you all of the time, people, and money you want. You won't always get it. But you should always see genuine effort and rationality. Its absence can be a symptom of a deeper issue, so if something doesn't make sense, try to discover the root cause. Understanding helps everyone, even if you can't do anything about it.

Silent Night

Focusing on the needs of the people involved in your project can pay tremendous dividends, especially when times get tough. And times will get tough.

The team was working feverishly to deliver a very large project integrating hundreds of programs, interfaces, and features. For months the project had been in Red status meaning late, low confidence, and high risk. A War Room was set up to coordinate testing 24 hours a day. Process and data flow posters papered the walls. Something was always not working. Activities were planned daily, and sometimes hourly.

As Christmas approached, long hours were the norm and the stress on the team was becoming apparent. The project leadership raised our concerns to management, and in response the Vice Presidents in charge of the project made an unprecedented demand. We called it "Silent Night."

From 3:00 in the afternoon on Christmas Eve until 8:00 in the morning the day after Christmas, no work was to be done by anyone. Period. No emails. No test cases. No phone calls. No anything.

This was not one of those disingenuous directives, like, "we know you need to enjoy your holiday, wink wink, so spend time with your family, wink wink, and if you just happen to catch up a little bit between eggnog, wink wink." No. They made it clear that they were very serious about the break and that any activity would be looked upon with extreme disfavor. Everyone. No exceptions.

Some were concerned about losing 40 hours of testing time, but the benefit to the project more than made up for the investment. Focus improved going into Christmas and the team returned renewed and reinvigorated. The next few

months were far from easy, but the product was
successfully delivered that Spring. This 40-hour break,
demonstrating management's sensitivity to the needs of
the team, was key to pushing through to the finish.

Finding Your Impossible Project

Ordinary Projects may be less impactful and less exciting, but they are also less risky and are invaluable for anyone aspiring to one day lead an Impossible Project. Use them to build your reputation for reliability and excellence.

Don't be discouraged if you don't get tapped to do an Impossible Project right away. Finding your Impossible Project takes equal parts preparation, anticipation, and luck. Approach every assignment as an opportunity to deliver something great.

While you are establishing your project delivery track record, cultivate relationships with SMEs and management throughout the company. One of your most valuable corporate assets is your network. But don't just be a leech. Find ways to help them, perhaps through projects that you help them to deliver. Also, find mentors and learn as much as you can from them.

Be actively curious about your company's needs, its pain points, and its strategic direction. Look for projects that support long-term objectives, that implement new capabilities or significantly improve existing ones, or that deliver new services or features that customers have been demanding. What perennial problems never seem to be solved? What new markets is the company looking to expand into? Some of this information is delivered periodically in the form of town hall meetings and shareholder reports. Ask around. You'll be amazed at what you can discover by simply showing interest.

When you find something that excites you, pounce on it.

Don't wait.

Be assertive.

Ask to lead it.

Lean into your track record, experience, and expertise, especially having read this book!! To awkwardly paraphrase Wayne Gretzky: you will never deliver any of the projects you don't lead. Maybe management had you in mind, but maybe they didn't know you were interested.

Besides asking and being asked, a third way to lead an Impossible Project is to initiate it yourself. This is probably the most challenging as well as the riskiest. Unless you have significant resources at your disposal or a very focused objective, the scope of your vision will likely exceed your capability to deliver. In this situation you are likely to be the lead as well as the subject matter expert and assuming both roles simultaneously is problematic. We'll cover that in the Fourth Secret. Instead, consider selling your idea to the appropriate stakeholders and then lead its implementation.

When a Project Devolves Into a Death March or Worse

Projects do sometimes become Death Marches. Now that you know how to identify them you can do your best to avoid them. But sometimes that's not an option.

I hate to have to mention it, but malicious intent does occasionally happen. A team or individual may be purposely set up for failure. Fortunately this is very rare. Even if demand is misaligned or the objective isn't clear or management isn't supportive, it is still overwhelmingly likely that they want you to succeed. Or at least deliver something.

You may already be too deeply entrenched when you find yourself in this situation. Transitioning off may be difficult, and abandoning ship may have negative career consequences.

Only you can weigh the liability of leaving against the liability of staying. You might be stuck. But just like being tapped to plan the department's holiday party (considered by many to be the least-desirable corporate assignment), this is also an opportunity. Just as an Impossible Project can devolve into a Death March, the latter can be rescued from the precipice.

Define objectives that can be successfully delivered. Be a steadying influence on your team. Again, it is beyond the scope of this book to provide a roadmap for salvaging a Death March. If you see that your project is moving in that direction and you are along for the ride, consult Yourdon's book. Seriously.

Finally, don't just survive, although that is certainly the minimum.

Thrive.

First Secret: Revealed

Recognize the Difference Between an Impossible Project and a Death March

- Intrinsic challenges are inherent to the problem itself and can include technical complexity and business process transformation.

- Impossible Projects are interesting and impactful, with high intrinsic difficulty and substantial benefit.

- Extrinsic challenges are imposed by outside forces and can include schedule, staff, budget, and scope constraints, as well as non-functional requirements.

- Death Marches have unnecessarily high extrinsic difficulty. They are usually the result of a misalignment or mismanagement that could be corrected if there was the will to do it.

- Ordinary Projects comprise the overwhelming majority of a company's efforts at any given time. Use them to cultivate your reputation and project delivery track record.

- When assessing a project, consider customer demand, customer clarity, and management support. All are required for success.

- Beware of projects where demand, benefit, and impact are not aligned, especially when the customer is negatively impacted.

- Actively seek out an Impossible Project to lead. When you find one, be assertive about getting involved.

Second Secret

Practice Relentless Pragmatism

Congratulations on your decision to lead an Impossible Project! And on finding one that looks promising. My experience is that while these projects are the most difficult they are also the most rewarding. The two probably go together. You're in for an adventure!

Before diving in, there's one more preliminary item to cover. You've got a critical decision to make. You would think that it would be committing to accomplishing the project, or delivering it on time and under budget, or something like that. You can probably hear yourself saying that to your boss or to the project sponsor, like you're making a head coach halftime locker-room speech. After all, by undertaking an Impossible Project you are endeavoring to defy the odds to accomplish something significant. You want to express your confidence, especially to yourself. But that's not it.

While delivery, budget, and timelines are important, even more important is making the intentional decision to be unwavering in your commitment to practical solutions. In other words:

Be relentlessly pragmatic.

Approach decisions objectively, not emotionally. This mindset is critical in an Impossible Project. See the project as it is, not as you want it to be. It's not always easy, especially as you become increasingly invested in the project and its success. This is where the "relentlessly" becomes necessary.

To be clear, this is not to suggest that you should be passionless, or that you should focus solely on the task at hand. Quite the opposite. In the next chapter we'll explore your role in sharing the project vision, and that leans heavily into inspiration and emotion.

Committing to pragmatism at the outset simplifies your job. You can say what needs to be said without censoring yourself. You will know what you have and what you need; where you are and where you're going.

Relentless pragmatism is also the best way to prevent your Impossible Project from inadvertently devolving into a Death March. Symptoms, like those covered in the previous chapter, are almost always apparent, but are too often ignored or downplayed in the interest of appearances.

Decision-making methodologies can help. SWOT,* Pareto,† and Cost-Benefit Analyses are indispensable tools. These techniques and many, many more are covered in myriad books, articles, and training courses. Their details are beyond our scope.

---

*SWOT (Strengths, Weaknesses, Opportunities, and Threats) is a technique for identifying and analyzing the internal and external factors that impact an organization's success.

† Pareto is a statistical technique used in decision making to identify the most significant factors that contribute to a particular outcome. It is often referred to as the 80/20 rule.

I would, however, like to share two concepts that have been helpful to me on multiple Impossible Projects. While they aren't decision-making frameworks *per se*, they provide a context for approaching problems and decisions. I will refer back to them often in subsequent chapters: The Quality Triangle, and Feasible → Preferable → Optimal.

The Quality Triangle

Odds are that you've seen the Quality Triangle diagram or something like it before. Perhaps it was called the Project Management Triangle, the Golden Triangle, or the Triangle of Quality. The vertex labels can vary but the concept is still the same: resources, scope, and time are all related, and collectively impact quality.

The Quality Triangle

Resources are the assets devoted to the project, and can be categorized into several different types:

Monetary: Funding allocated to the project used, for example, to purchase equipment, capitalize FTEs*, hire contractors and consultants, conduct training, and hold celebrations and recognitions.

Personnel: The people participating in the project having the required knowledge, experience, and expertise.

Informational: A company's most valuable asset is the collective knowledge contained not only in databases, spreadsheets, and documents, but also in its institutional memory which can include designs, processes, trade secrets, patents, culture, and general corporate know-how. The project team must include those with deep knowledge of these assets as well as the systems that produce and manage them.

Physical: The facilities, infrastructure, networking, raw materials, and natural resources required to host, support, and produce the end product.

Scope encompasses the project objectives and stakeholder expectations, including:

Deliverables: The set of tangible products and services produced to realize the business customer's vision.

Requirements: The set of specific functional and non-functional specifications and features.

Time is almost always given as the dates by which the business

---

*Full Time Equivalent employees

customer expects the completion of certain intermediate milestones and ultimately of the requested deliverables.

Quality is a little trickier. Everyone wants to deliver a high-quality product, but what specifically does that mean? Does it mean that all of the defects are eliminated before the product is released? That seems unlikely. Some defects are more consequential than others. Your business customer will play a critical role in evaluating the trade-off between resolving defects and releasing the product.

The power of the quality triangle is that it makes clear that a change in one dimension necessarily impacts the other three. The customer may want additional features. The project team may discover that it underestimated the development time. The databases may not contain the expected information. A component may not perform its function as expected, or may fail unexpectedly. A key participant may be reallocated to a different project. The Quality Triangle provides a framework for evaluating these changes.

For example, let's say the customer increases the scope of the project by demanding additional features. More resources and/or time must be provided to deliver the same quality. Too often in this scenario, though, it is quality that suffers. This may be because the consequences are not immediately apparent, or because of the irrational belief that *this* time, on *this* project, with *this* team, there won't be as many defects to sort out later and we'll make up the time at the end. Things usually don't work out that way.

When resources and time become constrained, negotiations almost always focus on scope. It has the greatest impact on the other dimensions and is usually the easiest to change. Within reason. Every Impossible Project I've worked has had at least one feature dropped–usually one of the least consequential–in the interest of successfully delivering the rest.

Finally, The Quality Triangle clearly illustrates importance of the partnership between management and business customer. Management provides the resources, often with the support of the customer. The business customer defines the scope, time, and quality with the advice of management. Any breakdown jeopardizes success.

Feasible → Preferable → Optimal

From the first moment you learn about the initiative that will become your Impossible Project, you will instinctively and reflexively start thinking about the solution. This thinking, working, and reworking in your head and on paper will continue throughout.

The second concept described in this chapter will help you to know where to start, and more importantly, to know when to stop. After all, as Toni Morrison famously said, "All art is knowing when to stop." And I strongly believe that there's no less art in system design and architecture as in building design and architecture. Elegance is a quality that is attainable in the solution to any problem in any field.

The idea is simple. Start with a solution. Any solution. A

feasible solution. Remember, we're not implementing anything yet, just working it out on paper (or as I prefer, the whiteboard). As you expand the project team, as you learn more, and as you exercise that solution you will discover that you can improve upon it. The result is *preferable* to the original. You can choose to continue to refine that solution, making it more elegant, more performant, more resilient, and more flexible. Eventually you will reach an *optimal* solution beyond which few additional reasonable enhancements exist.

A Cost-Benefit Analysis informs the decision to continue from feasible to preferable to optimal. I have found that refinement beyond the Feasible Solution is almost always necessary. On the other hand, squeezing out every last drop from a Preferable Solution usually leads to diminishing returns. Preferable is usually preferred.

Best of all, this approach applies at any scale, from the overall project all the way down to the individual component.

Feasible

Your goal at the outset is to solve the problem in any way possible. Take all the advice you can get.

Oftentimes those who requested the project will have ideas about how it should be implemented. They may have even mapped out a high-level system flow as part of their pre-project research. That's fine, as long as that's the first word on the subject, not the last.

The Feasible Solution will often represent a best guess based on your own knowledge of the business as well as of existing systems and processes. You probably haven't identified most of the project team members. You might not even know which areas will need to be represented. That's also fine. You'll work that out later.

A Feasible Solution might not be pretty or elegant. But it looks like it'll probably work. Data can find its way from Point A to Point B and the business objectives can be delivered. Finding a Feasible Solution is a significant milestone. It is one of the most exciting moments in the whole project. Morale is lifted and the team has new energy.

Your Impossible Project has become ... well ... feasible.

I Abhor "Minimum Viable Product"

Yes, I understand that's a strong statement, but it accurately captures my feelings about the concept. Well, not so much the concept itself. The idea is fine. The problem is the way that it is used. Or more accurately, misused.

The term, Minimum Viable Product, or MVP for short, was originally coined by Frank Robinson in 2001, and popularized by Eric Ries, developer of the Lean Startup Methodology, in 2009. The definition has evolved in many different directions over time, but MVP most often refers to the initial version of a product, delivered as quickly and with as little effort as possible, in order to collect feedback and test the product's potential so that subsequent development can be appropriately directed (or redirected).

Too often, though, MVP is used as an excuse to avoid resolving the hard implementation problems. They are simply jettisoned as no longer part of the Minimum Viable Product and thought about no more. That's OK if that deliverable is not important to the customer. But if it is, ignoring the problem will not make it go away. You may even end up making the problem more difficult by further constraining the eventual solution.

User experience should be the primary factor when considering project scope compromises. Removing a deliverable or feature because of design or implementation difficulty should be a last resort.

Preferable

Your Feasible Solution is just a start. Don't stop there. And for goodness sakes, don't send it to the developers to implement. All "feasible" means is that the problem can probably be solved. It's not the solution you want to deliver.

While developing the Feasible Solution, you identified areas where you'll need to engage additional SMEs. Impossible Projects have an inherent complexity that cannot be sorted out in an initial draft. Besides, it's easier for your team to start with a straw man than with a blank sheet of paper.

Each new participant will drill into their own domain. They will uncover constraints and fill in details. They will correct your invalid assumptions and simplify your complications.

It may take several iterations of the solution evolving over time, but the result will be a much improved *Preferable Solution.*

I have on occasion heard complaints that continuing past the Feasible Solution amounts to over-engineering. These are usually accompanied by an appeal to Minimum Viable Product, as in, "this will suffice as our MVP." I vehemently disagree. Do not conflate Feasible Solution and Minimum Viable Product. They are NOT the same. In fact, a Feasible Solution is not intended to be a product at all. At least not yet.

Pressing on to a Preferable Solution is about leveraging the collective experience and foresight of the team to produce something that won't just work but will work well. It's about the "abilities": adaptability, flexibility, usability, reliability, maintainability, scalability, and extendability. Don't be satisfied with expediency today that causes problems or sacrifices excellence tomorrow.

As you refine the design, focus disproportionately on making life easier for your customers and users. If that means simplifying the interface, then do it. If that means optimizing an internal calculation to decrease response time, then do it.

Again, conflicts will arise about whether to continue to refine certain parts of a Feasible Solution. You may recognize that the solution isn't very good, but some other party, usually the impacted team, may disagree. Some companies have a customer quality review team to arbitrate, but usually management decides. Either way, the most you can do is to make your case, articulate the pros and cons of each approach, and then let them decide. That's their job.

If you do get stuck with a solution that is substantively flawed, document your concerns constructively and in writing, and include the corrective actions in the list of future enhancements. Yes, it's a bit of butt-covering, but you don't want to get blamed for an inartful design once the project is delivered. That said, it is also your responsibility to make it work. Whatever the decision. It is not worth jeopardizing your project just to prove a point. Nobody will care that you were right. You will be going down on that same sinking ship.

The additional effort to improve from feasible to preferable is almost always worth it. When the cost of making additional refinements, or even searching for them, exceeds the potential benefit, you have found your stopping place.

Optimal

The boundaries between feasible, preferable, and optimal are admittedly subjective. One person's Preferable Solution might be another's Optimal Solution.

While most of us are not developing open heart surgery procedures or manned rocket ship controllers, certain key components in our projects may have critical resource, quality, availability, or performance requirements. Then, the effort to squeeze out those remaining improvements is justified.

Ultimately, it depends on the potential for refinement, the cost/benefit tradeoff, and management and the customer's acceptable threshold for the "abilities."

—

One final note. In projects using an agile methodology, there's a temptation to start implementation before design and architecture are completed. This can be a very bad thing for an Impossible Project. Especially one that is very large and/or very complex. The overall architecture and data flow must be at least mostly finalized as part of the architecture runway. Changes impact too many systems to allow the architecture to be "emergent." Too many changes will inevitably lead to a Death March.

Learning from Failure

I first developed the Feasible → Preferable → Optimal concept when I was in graduate school teaching Introductory Computer Science. The class was working through the book Programming Pearls *by Jon Bentley. It covered programming design principles and encouraged developers to go beyond the initial, obvious approaches to produce more efficient and elegant solutions.*

One of the assignments was to, "Write a 'banner' procedure that takes the word HELLO as input and produces as output an array of asterisks five lines high that graphically depicts that word." Something like:

```
*    *    ****    *        *          ***
*    *    *       *        *        *     *
****      ****    *        *        *     *
*    *    *       *        *        *     *
*    *    ****    ****     *****     ***
```

It looks so primitive, but at the time laser printers were so expensive a college Computer Science department might only have a couple. Most assignments were turned in on dot-matrix printouts where you had to tear off the tractor feed strips on each side. Nevertheless, the concepts are just as applicable today as they were back then.

I also gave the class two hints. First, the assignment should take about an hour to complete and if it takes less they should think more deeply about their solution. Second, follow-up assignments should take them less than a minute to complete if they did the first one correctly.

Most of the class hard-coded the five lines of output:

```
print "*   *  ****  *    *    ***"
print "*   *  *     *    *   *   *"
...
```

A few figured out that each letter could be implemented as its own subroutine, appending five hard-coded strings to five output buffers as each letter of the input word was read. (There are many ways to do this, but this approach was consistent with the concepts presented in the book.)

The follow-up assignment was to generate a banner that said "HAPPY BIRTHDAY." For those in the latter group, all that was required was to change the input word.

Disappointingly, most students simply hard-coded five new lines of output that spelled "HAPPY BIRTHDAY." I can't believe that any of them finished in less than a minute. Although the programs strictly satisfied the output requirements, it took a little more foresight and thinking to come up with an extendable solution.

Also disappointingly, very few of the students absorbed the point of the assignment. I consider that to be a failure on my part. We went back and reviewed the chapter, the techniques presented, and the assignment. It went a little better the second time.

But I got thinking about their initial solutions. The hard-coded output lines produced the desired output. It was a Feasible Solution, and it would have been fine if they never had to touch the program again. The follow-up assignment *encouraged them to push through to find a better, Preferable Solution.*

I used the same approach for my dissertation research. It took a long time to get the algorithms I was developing to perform correctly. I was relieved when they did. I finally had a Feasible Solution, even though it wasn't very elegant. I then analyzed each of the components to find improvements and with some effort produced a Preferable Solution. I could have continued to refine it into an Optimal Solution, but I wanted to graduate so I stopped. Those ideas made up the section entitled "Topics for Future Research."

Second Secret: Revealed

Practice Relentless Pragmatism

- Be unwavering in your commitment to practical solutions, approaching decisions objectively, not emotionally.

- Use the Quality Triangle as a framework to evaluate resource, scope, time, and quality requirements, as well as the ways that changes to one dimension impacts the others.

- Inform decisions with cost/benefit analyses.

- If you're going to invoke Minimum Viable Product, use it correctly as a rapid feedback mechanism and not an excuse to avoid the hard problems.

- Start with a Feasible Solution that demonstrates that the problem can be solved. Refine it into a Preferable Solution. This is probably where you'll stop. Continue to an Optimal Solution only if the additional effort is justified.

- You are not going to prevail in all design and architecture disagreements. While it's important to document your concerns, do not let any disappointment diminish your commitment to successful project delivery.

Third Secret

Clearly Articulate the Mission

Find a compilation of great speeches and read them. You'll notice a common characteristic: they almost always articulate a crystal clear vision of an aspirational future. Here are just a few examples from those collected by historian Simon Sebag Montefiore:[*]

> Martin Luther King, Jr. dreamt of a day when children of all races could play together.

> Indira Gandhi emphasized the importance of educated women to the future of India.

> George S. Patton rallied his troops to victory on the eve of D-Day.

> George W. Bush promised justice for those killed by terrorists.

> Jesus assured those that suffered for His sake would be blessed.

As the leader of an Impossible Project, it is up to you to articulate a crystal clear vision of an aspirational future to your team. Show them the results expected to be realized through

---

[*]Montefiore, Simon Sebag. *Speeches that Changed the World*. New York: Metro Books, 2013.

their efforts. Be committed and passionate about what they will accomplish.

Fortunately, you don't have to be a great speechwriter or a great orator. The key is clarity.

It all begins with understanding your customer's vision.

Aligning With Your Customer

Before engaging your team. Before developing a project plan. Before entering epics, features, and user stories into your SAFe Agile tool. Before doing anything else, align with your customer on the initiative's vision and objectives. They have been thinking about the project for some time prior to your involvement. They know the *what* and the *why*. You need to come up to speed with them.

Throughout the project, every activity and deliverable must support the vision. If it doesn't, ask yourself and your customer whether that deliverable belongs in the project, or alternatively, whether the vision is sufficiently inclusive.

Once you and your customer are in sync with the vision, you can develop some related assets that will help you to communicate about the project: the elevator pitch, bumper sticker, key features, and personas and scenarios. Your customer may already have some or all of these. If not, then now is the time to start.

The Elevator Pitch and Bumper Sticker

Projects often begin as a bullet list of features. You'll need one of those soon, but don't start there. Instead, and as trite as it might sound, start with the project's vision or mission. Answer the question: "What are you working on?"

You've got fifteen seconds. One floor on the elevator with the CEO. An acquaintance fly-by at a cocktail party. Twenty-five words. Any longer than that and you risk losing your audience.

It is the inspirational North Star. The elevator pitch is part of many project initiation packages and may already exist for yours. If not, create one. Perhaps something like:

> A smart store that allows shoppers to place items into their cart, pay, and leave without stopping at a checkout counter.

> A conversational medical assistant application that uses artificial intelligence to interpret symptoms and test results, and to suggest diagnoses.

> Improving teamwork through a common, intentional culture that focuses on a set of key interpersonal tenets.

Then, go one step farther and boil down the elevator pitch into a one to four word bumper sticker:

> Skip the Checkout

> AI-Based Medical Diagnosis

> Shared Culture, Shared Values

Have some bumper stickers, buttons, or magnets printed and distribute them to your project team, customers, and management. I still have several from projects that I worked on, and I've seen some that found their way onto what seemed like every cubicle wall in the company.

Spectacularly Uninspiring

One of my early projects failed due to the absence of an articulated vision.

The team had just delivered a large project. As users began to fully exercise the system, the need for certain additional capabilities as well as for the refinement of existing capabilities became clear. They were accumulated into a long list, organized, and prioritized.

While everybody recognized their importance, a project consisting of a seemingly never-ending feature parade fell flat. It lacked a unifying idea or concept. There was no vision to rally around and propel the project forward.

As a result, the team moved on to other projects and this effort was dropped. In time, many of the items on the list were implemented. But looking back on it now, the delivery of those capabilities could have been accelerated had they been subordinated to an overarching vision instead of the other way around.

Key Objectives

Once the vision is clear, create a bullet list of high-level objectives. I repeat, high-level. In practice these are often interchangeably referred to as project features or deliverables. A small group could spend an entire evening over dinner and drinks debating the nuances of these terms. For our purposes here, features and deliverables are the next level of detail under each objective.

In my experience, even the largest projects should have no more than about eight key objectives. Smaller projects might only have one or two. I'd be willing to bet that they've already been documented for your project. They're probably what attracted you to it in the first place. They're the deliverables that you and your team will rally around and get excited about.

At the beginning of the project, they detail "What we are going to do." Throughout the project they provide structure to "What we are doing." At the end of the project, they are "What we did."

Hundreds of books, articles, and websites have been written about requirements elicitation and feature writing. It may be worth checking some out. In short, well-articulated objectives are written from the customer's perspective, and are specific, measurable, achievable, and aligned to the vision.

Make sure that you are clear about each objective. Ask questions until you understand completely. Do your best to keep your brain out of problem-solving mode. Stick with the *what* and avoid the *how*. For now. And learn from my mistake and avoid letting the key objectives become a "To Do" list.

Personas and Scenarios

A *persona* is a fictional representation of a set of target customers described by certain demographic and/or behavioral characteristics. A *scenario* is a story built around a persona that illustrates their interactions with the project deliverables.

Personas and scenarios communicate project objectives by bringing the features to life, humanizing the customers, helping the team relate to the customers' needs and struggles, and keeping the team focused on the customer's perspective. Personas and scenarios are identified very early in the project, and are often essential for getting it approved. Don't be surprised if the project sponsor has already written several.

In addition, they are valuable feature filters. If nobody can articulate who's going to use a feature, why they would use it, and how they would use it, then that feature probably hasn't been thought through fully and may not be needed. This is a red flag. Work with the project sponsor to develop personas and scenarios for that feature, or remove it from the project.

Take it as a challenge to find situations or twists that may not have been considered. Develop new personas and scenarios. Imagine what could go wrong, what could break, or how the product could be used improperly. They say that nothing is ever foolproof because fools are so ingenious. Rise to that challenge. Be creative.

A New Grocery Store Service

Grocery store online ordering with curbside pickup is ubiquitous today, but at some point a product innovation team was tasked with exploring the idea. They no doubt imagined who would use this new service and how. Maybe it looked something like this:

Persona: Janet is a young parent with three small children. She does not have time between school drop-off in the morning and pick-up in the afternoon for grocery shopping. As a result, a trip to the store with the kids can be stressful. She enjoys shopping at BuyMore Market, but making it through the store without a meltdown is a challenge. Somebody is always crying by the time they are ready to leave. Sometimes it's Janet herself.

Scenario: In the evening, after the children have gone to bed, Janet selects the groceries she needs using the new BuyMore Online phone app. Since her previous choices were saved, she can quickly assemble a basket full of her usual items. Payment is made and the order is scheduled for pickup. The next afternoon Janet collects her children, makes her way to the store, and pulls into a designated parking space. She sees that she received a text message notifying her that her order is ready. She replies to the message indicating that she has arrived. Her groceries are brought out to the car and placed into the trunk. Shopping is done for the week, and neither she nor her children had to leave the car. And nobody is crying.

Aligning With Management

Very early in my career, I was chatting with a mentor about project engagement. She commented that the higher the management level, the earlier they become involved with a project (or are at least aware of it), and the longer they remain with it. This means that by the time you join, management is probably already on board.

Management support expectations were detailed with the First Secret. All of those questions should now be satisfactorily answered. You know their expectations of your role and you know that they are committed to the project. You have clarity on funding, team member participation, prioritization, timeframes, and advocacy.

Expand the common understanding of project objectives that now exists between you and the customer to include management. If the customer and management have been working together on the project for a while, that alignment may already exist. Nevertheless, it is worth probing a little bit to prevent confusion later. Ask management to share their understanding with you. If all three parties are on the same page, then you can be pretty sure that you are good to proceed.

Aligning the Project Team - The Kick-Off Meeting

Clearly and continually articulating the project mission is one of the most important services you provide to your team. You are the one they look to first for direction, leadership, and consistency. Especially when things get difficult.

The Fourth Secret covers assembling your team. You may want to skip ahead and read that chapter before continuing. Or not. Either way works.

For now, let's assume that they've been gathered and are ready to start. That means a kick-off meeting! Or as a friend calls them, "Slides and Sandwiches." When done correctly, this event sets a positive and confident tone for the entire project.

By the end of the meeting, each team member should be:

Aligned with you, management, and the customer regarding project vision and objectives.

Able to articulate the project vision and objectives to others.

This section steps you through the meeting and its content, and provides some tips for maximizing its effectiveness. A sample agenda is provided at the end of this chapter.

Someone Else Starts the Meeting

That seems like an odd point to emphasize, but the reason will become apparent shortly. Your customer is the best candidate for this job. They should be in the room with you anyway to show support and unity. They can also provide a first-hand perspective on the problem being solved as well as a face for the customer.

They begin by welcoming the team to the project and to the meeting, and by introducing themself and their role. Then introductions of the project leadership, including you. Sometimes one or more upper management sponsors will attend, or at least be there at the beginning to say a few words.

None of these introductory speakers should get into any of the specific features of the project itself.

Don't mix the preliminaries with the particulars.

Acknowledge that while those in the room will have varying

levels of familiarity with the project details, by the end of the meeting everyone will have a common understanding.

This is the time to cover housekeeping details like the agenda, restroom location, and lunch plans. Some companies have standard pre-meeting rituals like safety briefings or culture reinforcement. The point is to get everything else out of the way before you speak.

That takes care of the preliminaries. Time for you to address your whole team for the first time. You're on!!

Start With the Vision

**In any presentation or speech,
your very first words are the most important.**

You have your audience's maximum attention and maximum curiosity. Unfortunately, most speakers squander this opportunity on introductions and housekeeping. That's why someone else should launch the meeting.

By now you have your elevator speech down pat. Start there. Articulate the vision. Paint the verbal picture of the future. Describe how the world will be a better place when the project is finished.

Let your team see your passion for the project. They will take their cues from you. If you are excited, optimistic, and enthusiastic they will be, too. Similarly if you are disinterested, pessimistic, or apathetic.

Speak without slides.

If you need to have something on the screen behind you, use an image overlaid with the bumper sticker description of the project. In any speech, my target is at most six words per slide.

The reason is that your audience cannot both read and listen at the same time. You must therefore decide, at each point in your presentation, whether you want them reading your slides or listening to you. Populate your slides accordingly. Right now you want them to be focused on what you're saying.

Everything is Clearer in Your Own Head

Sometimes what seems perfectly clear to you is incomprehensible to others. Try this little game.

Find a partner. Think of a simple, child's song that everybody should know. Something like Baa Baa Black Sheep, Happy Birthday, or Twinkle Twinkle Little Star. Tap the rhythm of the song into the palm of your partner's hand and ask them to name that tune. They usually cannot.

You hear the song perfectly in your own mind's ear. The message you're sending (the taps) is being received, but the information you're trying to send (the specific song) is not. Just because it's clear to you, doesn't mean that it's clear to your partner. The only time I've seen a partnership successfully guess the song is when both thought of the same song at the beginning of the exercise and the receiver was already thinking of it when the tapping started.

Take yourself out of your own head when you are developing and later practicing your presentation. Try to view your content from the perspective of someone who doesn't know anything about the project. Ask for help with the messaging from your customer, or better yet from a friend who is working on something different.

When I was in graduate school, my research explored the application of genetic algorithms to the development of fuzzy logic controllers. My dissertation began not with math or computer programs but with a story about a refrigerator that may or may not have an apple inside.

I wanted the concepts to be understandable to readers who weren't familiar with those topics. I sent draft versions to friends and family members and asked them if after reading the introductory chapter they felt like they had at least a basic understanding. I continued to refine the text until the answer to that question was yes.

Objectives, Personas, and Scenarios

Some presenters will talk through a single slide containing a list of all the project objectives, while others prefer to reveal them one at a time. Remember that if you display them all at once, your audience will spend the first minute or two reading the slide and not listening to you. That's not necessarily a problem, you just have to remember not to say anything important during that minute or two.

And for goodness sake, don't just read the text on the slides one line after another from top to bottom.

My preference is to boil each objective down to a one-to-four word title, then present a list of those titles. Your audience can consume that information quickly and then tune back into you for the details. The titles are also useful throughout the project as update and status report section headings.

Personas and scenarios present a somewhat greater challenge.

Since they're already in story form, it's tempting to paste them onto the slides. Don't do this. You'll create an impenetrable wall of text that's not pleasant for your audience and probably not much fun for you either.

Instead, construct the slide using a picture that represents the persona along with some bullet points describing who they are and what they are trying to accomplish. You can still read the prose if you want, I suppose, just don't put it on the slide.

The Earlier Persona and Scenario Example as a Slide

Questions and Introductions

You've covered a lot of ground and given the team a lot to think about. Now stop. Take questions about the vision, objectives, personas and scenarios. Defer project management questions like timelines and resources. You'll get to those shortly. Allocate plenty of time for questions. Ask somebody to capture items to cover later (often referred to as "parking lot" items). Keep in mind that the goal is to align the project team with the vision already shared by the customer, management, and you.

Be suspicious if you don't get any or many questions. It's tempting to believe that you did such a great job that everyone is completely aligned and on board. More likely they're overwhelmed, sitting in stunned silence.

The next item on the agenda, introductions, will move the meeting past any unintended tranquility. But hold on. We've been going for nearly an hour. Shouldn't this have been done earlier? Like when the project leadership was introduced?

No. By now, everyone should have at least a cursory understanding of the project and their place in it. Ask each team member to introduce themselves:

Name, role, group/department.

How do they see their area fitting into the project?

Which objectives do they expect to help deliver?

Display a slide showing the list of objectives throughout this activity for reference.

Emphasize that it's OK if they don't precisely know their place yet. Maybe it's all new and not entirely clear to them. Maybe you thought that their area would need to participate, but perhaps they don't. Assign someone to record each person's answer. This is valuable information. Follow up individually later as needed to close any gaps.

Project Management Details

Conclude the meeting with a very brief overview of the key project management details. Emphasis on brief. The team has enough to digest. If your project has a dedicated project manager, have them cover this section. Include a high-level timeline, initial status meeting cadence, and immediate next steps. At this point you might only have the final target date without any defined milestones. That's OK. Work breakdown details, issue tracking procedures, status report formats, communication plans, budget allocation, and expense request processes are all subjects for future meetings.

Finally, create cubicle wall art with the project objectives and distribute it to the team at the end of the meeting. It can be a list or an infographic or a screen saver or anything. Be creative. Whatever you create should be visible as a reference throughout the project. It could also be used as a framework for status meeting reports and for organizing agile teams. At the end of the project you will be able to go through each objective and show how it was delivered.

Meeting adjourned.

Keeping the Conversation On Track

Like you, your team will instinctively begin solutioning as soon as they start seeing the objectives. Chasing these rabbits is easy and fun, but it is a distraction in your kick-off meeting. Brainstorming with the team will come soon. Just not now. Whenever the conversation drifts toward the *how*, acknowledge the idea, adding it to the parking lot of necessary, then return to the *what*.

Another alluring conversational sinkhole is worrying about potential problems, roadblocks, and issues. There are a million ways for an Impossible Project to fail. Don't allow the meeting to devolve into a downward spiral of "can't." Again, acknowledge the concern, make a note of it if necessary, and move on.

One of the worst case scenarios for your kick-off meeting is reaching the end and discovering that, for whatever reason, your message didn't resonate with the team. Everything was clear in your own head but it just didn't connect. Maybe you need more clarity about the objectives yourself, or maybe you need different messaging. Solicit feedback and advice from other meeting participants to uncover where the breakdown occurred. You may end up trying again later either individually or collectively. It's not what you want to do, but aligning with your team is that important.

Uncertainty and Complexity

The opposite of clarity is uncertainty. Uncertainty generates complexity. Complexity increases difficulty. And you don't need to make your Impossible Project any more difficult than it already is.

Uncertainty can be intrinsic or extrinsic, just like the difficulties discussed with the First Secret. Intrinsic uncertainty is inherent to the project. You won't have much if any control over it. The best you can do is to recognize it and develop contingencies.

Consider the simple question of when to head to the airport for a departing flight. How much traffic will you encounter at that time of day? What are the weather and road conditions? Will you be able to park in a nearby lot or will you have to wait for the bus to bring you in from two miles away? How long are the lines at baggage check and security? All of these uncertainties factor into that single decision of when to leave. But even then you can't plan for everything. You might get into an accident or have engine trouble. Someone else might get into an accident that closes the road in front of you. You might run over a nail and get a flat tire. You might notice that the goat escaped from her pen and is wandering around in the woods, and there's nobody else at home to retrieve her.

The same challenges apply to software development, system integration, and really any project. It would be easy if everything always worked the way it's supposed to: the users always enter the data correctly, the sensors never fail, and the other groups' programs always function properly. But we can't count on any of that. What do we do if the product code entered by the customer is not in the database? What if a sensor stops communicating? What if the data transmission is corrupted? Anticipate as many potential anomalies as possible, and develop contingencies for each. Of course, each contingency increases the complexity. And even then you can't foresee everything.

On the other hand, extrinsic uncertainty is like a cancer that spreads through a project causing churn, dissatisfaction, and delay. Fortunately, you can control extrinsic uncertainty, and its two main sources in particular.

The first is the appearance of misalignment among the project leadership. Disagreements will happen. This is normal. In fact, if there weren't any disagreements, I'd be worried that we weren't thinking hard enough or exploring alternatives seriously enough. But conduct those conversations privately and resolve them before exposing any changes to the rest of the team. It may turn out that the problem you thought you had didn't really exist. Don't unnecessarily distract the team.

The second is changing project objectives. Imagine that for the past week you've been working heads-down to deliver a certain feature. It's nearly finished when you're told that its functionality is changing or is no longer needed. What is that going to do to your morale and sense of accomplishment? Certainly nothing good. An Impossible Project requires a lot of discretionary effort from everybody on the team. Don't undermine motivation by wasting the team's efforts.

When the objectives change frequently and seemingly arbitrarily, the team will not know day-to-day whether they are working on something that will make it into the finished product. "I'll wait to work on this until I know that it's really needed." Design decisions and implementation will be delayed, ultimately jeopardizing the final delivery date.

Change is Inevitable

OK. So, if change is inevitable, what can you do?

**First and foremost, ensure that
the project vision remains constant.**

Always. That's why we spent so much time earlier validating it and aligning the objectives to it. The impact of a change to the vision will ripple throughout every corner of the project. The entire project may need to be rethought, and it may be easier to start over from scratch.

Nevertheless, it is unrealistic to expect no changes to the objectives and features from conception to delivery, especially for a large project. A feature thought to be essential at the outset may no longer be needed, or may no longer be as critical. The technology required to support it may be discovered to be more expensive to purchase or to develop than expected.

Change is particularly common within the context of an agile development methodology. In fact, a key characteristic of agile is that the customer interacts directly with the project team, making adjustments as necessary throughout. That's a good thing. But it's tempting to fall back on "emergent design" to avoid thinking very deeply about the high-level architecture and key objectives at the beginning of the project. This is a mistake, and can lead to an otherwise manageable Impossible Project becoming a Death March.

The use of an agile methodology is not an excuse for ongoing changes to the project vision, objectives, features, or architecture.

Specific application requirements may evolve. The implementation details of the interfaces, data, and data model certainly will. But it doesn't matter whether you're using waterfall or agile or some other methodology, the vision must remain constant.

As the project progresses, changes may be required due to:

evolving or emerging business needs,

shifting business landscape or market conditions, and/or

insights gained during development and stakeholder feedback.

Feature deprioritization and elimination most often happens as milestone dates approach or when an analysis of the current project progress suggests that a delivery date is at risk. The Quality Triangle introduced with the Second Secret is particularly useful for understanding the trade-offs between cost, scope, time, and quality. The adjustments needed to bring those factors back into balance inform the path forward.

As a leader, it is useful for you to understand why the change is being considered, even if you were not consulted initially. Did the customer's requirements change? Is there a time or resource constraint? Did we get negative feedback about the customer experience? Determine the impact of the change, then communicate it to your customer and management so that they fully informed before a decision is finalized.

When eliminating or changing a feature, it's easy to become fixated on the effort that has already been devoted to its development. It's certainly a potential morale and motivation issue. While those factors should be considered, don't fall into the sunk cost trap. This is the tendency to let emotions regarding past investments drive the decision to continue down the same path. Instead, make the decision based on future costs and benefits.

Here are some questions to consider when eliminating or changing a feature:

> How much effort remains to deliver the feature?
>
> Can resources be added or the schedule adjusted to accommodate the change instead of eliminating the feature?
>
> Can the change be defined in a way that isolates its impact?
>
> Does the change in one feature impact other features?

What about adding a new feature? Scope expansion is always difficult because the project was resourced for the original feature set and there usually isn't a whole lot of excess capacity. Especially on an Impossible Project.

Some questions to ask when adding a feature:

> How much incremental effort will be required?
>
> Can existing features leverage the new one, thereby reducing their own effort?
>
> Can the new feature leverage existing assets?
>
> Is an adjustment to the underlying architecture required?
>
> Is the engagement of additional teams required?
>
> In the absence of additional resources, what current work will be deprioritized to accommodate the new feature?

Once the change has been finalized, share the details and impacts with the team. Expect to receive some push-back. You might not have been fully on board when you first heard about the change either. But it's your job to rip the bandage off and orient your team forward. Don't look back. Don't spend time relitigating. The team will follow your example. Frame the change as an opportunity, not an adversity. Demonstrate flexibility. Intransigence can be just as damaging to a project as uncertainty.

Sample Kick-Off Meeting Agenda

Preliminaries (Customer)
- Welcome
- Management Welcome
- Project Leadership Introductions
- Agenda Overview and Housekeeping

Project Overview (You)
- Vision
- Objectives
- Personas and Scenarios
- Questions
- Team Introductions

Project Management Overview (Project Manager)
- High-Level Timeline
- Status Meeting Cadence
- Next Steps

Third Secret: Revealed

Clearly Articulate the Mission

- Clarity and consistency are the best ways to prevent your Impossible Project from devolving into a Death March.

- Align with your customer and with management on the initiative's objectives.

- Develop your fifteen-second elevator pitch, personas and scenarios, and a short list of key features.

- Ensure that your project team is aligned with you on the initiative's objectives.

- Hold a kick-off meeting to communicate the vision, objectives, personas, and scenarios to your team.

- Remember that your audience cannot read slides and listen to you speak at the same time.

- While change is inevitable, minimize the number of changes and the impact of each.

Fourth Secret

Cast a Wide Net

The success of your Impossible Project largely depends upon the composition of your team and your ability to get the most out of them. This chapter covers assembling that team, identifying your most important team member, and getting started together.

Lead or Subject Matter Expert but Not Both

This is a very easy trap to fall into. After all, you probably rose to your present leadership position by becoming the subject matter expert (SME) for your domain. You no doubt know how that domain fits into the overall project, and what that part of the solution looks like. Plus, representing your own domain means one less team member that you, or your boss, have to recruit. Don't do it.

Don't try to be both lead and subject matter expert.

The most common type of Impossible Project is one that spans subject, operational, and/or application areas. Each will have its own SMEs that you will need to call upon to help design and develop the solution. Lean into their expertise.

When you're an expert, you come with tremendous context and expertise, but all of that works against you in a lead role. It's easy to make assumptions or to gloss over potentially significant details. I refer to this as being *contaminated with experience.*

It's also easy to disproportionately focus on the familiar area over more important areas, as well as over your leadership of the project as a whole. Maybe you are the top domain expert or application developer in the company, but understand that for you time spent coding is time not spent leading.

Add your backup to your team. The alternative is to step down as lead so that you can focus on the SME role.

Consider a modern battle tank with a crew consisting of a driver, gunner, loader, and commander. The commander is responsible for the soldiers and the vehicle: directing operations, making tactical decisions, coordinating with peers, and receiving orders and intelligence from headquarters. The other crew members have their own tasks, and the result is a smoothly operating unit. Now, it is likely that the commander is capable of doing all of the other jobs. Maybe the commander was one of the Army's best gunners. But while performing the gunner's role, the commander cannot assess the overall situation, direct operations, or coordinate communications, which puts the tank and everyone in it at greater risk. The commander must therefore maintain a broader scope and awareness for the good of the crew and of the mission.

The same is true for you and your team.

The Big Box Diagram

They say that if you give any kind of technical architect a whiteboard and dry-erase marker, the first thing they'll do is draw a box. Maybe a couple boxes connected by some lines and arrows. It's reflexive. It certainly is for me. A few more boxes, lines, and arrows and you have what I call the Big Box Diagram. A *Big Box Diagram* illustrates the high-level solution components and their relationships, and is the first step toward discovering and documenting the solution for your Impossible Project.

I come from the "Hello World" school of application development, where every program starts out as a few lines of code that displays "Hello World" on the screen. Features are incrementally added, but the key is to always have a functioning program. The same approach works for architecture development. I start most every project with a Big Box Diagram that represents the current working solution concept. It's also a way for me to capture and organize my understanding of the solution.

Begin by identifying the high-level solution components. You may not know many (or any) of the system, interface, or data details. Don't worry. Just write functional descriptions. Your first draft will probably look like a flowchart containing a sort of architectural analog of pseudocode.*

Leverage the resources that you have, starting with your customer. They may be familiar with the groups that

---

* Pseudocode is a description of the steps in an algorithm or computer program written using human-readable statements rather than technical syntax. These statements are often used as placeholders that provide context and direction during development.

participated in delivering similar projects in the past. They may even have sketched their ideas of what a solution would look like. I've found that some business teams like to dabble in solution architecture. That's not a problem at the outset, but you take it from there.

Some companies incorporate business process modeling into the project evaluation process. If yours does, the Business Architecture team can be a great resource. A business process model includes process flow, roles and responsibilities, inputs and outputs, decision points, and dependencies. While not a data flow or implementation map, it can inform the high-level components of both.

Each square (or rectangle) in your Big Box Diagram has inputs and outputs, and performs some function. I prefer to work from the outside in, starting with the capability being delivered at the bottom, the set of triggering events at the top, and then identifying the adjacent process steps until they meet in the middle.

As the solution evolves, always follow where the data or process path leads. Don't make any assumption. Make sure that each component receives all of the input it needs. This often requires that data from multiple upstream sources be composed, or integrated, before it can be used. It is tempting for one component to ask, or demand, that an upstream source integrate the data even though that source doesn't require all of that data itself. Step in and do not permit this to happen. It is axiomatic that data should be received from as close to its originating source as possible. Each pass-through system increases that distance, increases complexity, and complicates future enhancements and maintenance.

When starting with capability delivery and working backwards, ask at each step:

> What is the desired outcome or output?
>
> What are its prerequisites?
>
> What information is required?
>
> Where does that prerequisite information come from?
>
> How does that information get from where it is to where it needs to be?

Ask a similar set of questions when starting with the triggering events and working forwards:

> What initiates the process?
>
> What information is available from existing sources?
>
> What new information is required? From where?
>
> Can an existing interface be modified or must a new interface be created?

Experience suggests that the first iteration of this diagram will bear only the slightest resemblance to the roadmap that it will evolve into. I've gone back and looked at a few of my initial Big Box Diagrams and without exception they are embarrassingly simplistic and naïve. But they were a start and each improved over time. And right now it's more important to be fast than right.

Note that while the discussion of Big Box Diagrams here has focused on system development, this technique is applicable to any project in any domain that requires the composition and sequencing of multiple process steps.

Starting A Big Box Diagram

Your company may have an existing standard architecture development tool that can facilitate the creation and refinement of your Big Box Diagram. If so, great. Use it. I guess I'm a little low-tech because I've only ever used Visio. Version control, documentation, and relationship management take a little more effort, but I made it work.

Let's return to the grocery store curbside pickup example introduced in the previous chapter. From the scenario we can see that the solution appears to have four key components: order creation, scheduling, order picking, and order delivery. There will be more, but this gets us started.

Here is what the initial Big Box Diagram might look like:

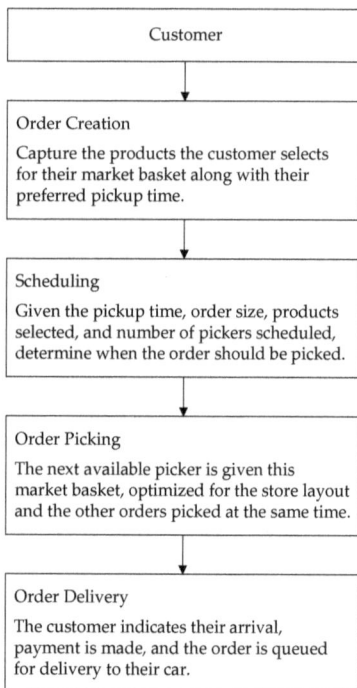

```
┌─────────────────────────────────────────┐
│                 Customer                  │
└─────────────────────────────────────────┘
                     │
                     ▼
┌─────────────────────────────────────────┐
│ Order Creation                            │
│ Capture the products the customer selects │
│ for their market basket along with their  │
│ preferred pickup time.                     │
└─────────────────────────────────────────┘
                     │
                     ▼
┌─────────────────────────────────────────┐
│ Scheduling                                │
│ Given the pickup time, order size,        │
│ products selected, and number of pickers  │
│ scheduled, determine when the order        │
│ should be picked.                          │
└─────────────────────────────────────────┘
                     │
                     ▼
┌─────────────────────────────────────────┐
│ Order Picking                             │
│ The next available picker is given this   │
│ market basket, optimized for the store    │
│ layout and the other orders picked at     │
│ the same time.                             │
└─────────────────────────────────────────┘
                     │
                     ▼
┌─────────────────────────────────────────┐
│ Order Delivery                            │
│ The customer indicates their arrival,     │
│ payment is made, and the order is queued  │
│ for delivery to their car.                 │
└─────────────────────────────────────────┘
```

These components can be decomposed into a set of customer-facing interface functions that drive capability delivery. We can also start to identify some of the required data repositories and shared services. We're not necessarily identifying specific systems right now. It's best not to make assumptions at the outset. On the other hand, if it is clear that, for example, the Concierge Guest Management System (CGMS) is the corporate customer information source, then go ahead and show it.

Let's take a closer look at Market Basket Selections which is a feature under Order Creation.

The Customer accesses the Market Basket Selections interface, which requires Product and Customer data. The result is the creation of an Order, which triggers Payment Processing, Order Picking, and Picker Scheduling. And so forth.

Here's a very rough next Big Box Diagram iteration:

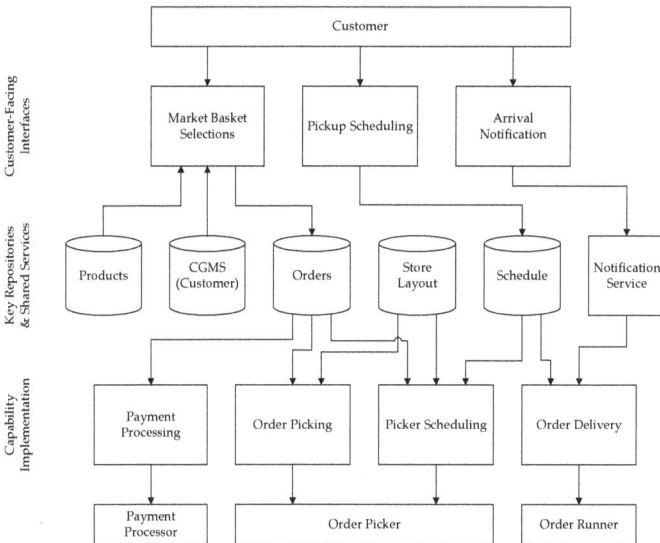

It's messy, almost certainly incorrect, and most definitely incomplete. Nevertheless, a lot of information is already packed into this single picture.

From this starting point, the next steps, or at least the questions that lead you to the next steps become clear. For starters: Which of these components already exist and do they contain the required data?

Over time, the diagram will become much more detailed and much more correct as you work with your team to develop the solution.

Assembling Your Team

Once you start drilling into the Big Boxes, you will need to find experts who can provide additional details about system capabilities and functionalities. The cast of characters becomes apparent pretty quickly.

You're not asking for these experts to be assigned to the project. Not yet. For now you just need advice and answers to a few questions. You're still doing preliminary research to establish a baseline understanding of the problem and the potential components of a solution.

I became an expert at getting time in the margins with SMEs to learn about their systems and to assess their potential involvement in my projects. A half-hour or so here and there. A lunchtime meeting works well, especially when you're buying. Be appreciative and never take for granted or abuse their willingness to chat.

This is how you identify your team.

Once you have a general solution outline, make your requests for team members. Reach out to everybody you can think of that could be impacted. Bring them on board, or at least notify them that they might be needed.

Some leads like to start with a small team and expand it as necessary, but I prefer the opposite. I find that it's easier to pare down a large team as the solution comes into focus than it is to discover that you are missing a key participant and have to track them down and onboard them later.

This is where establishing a common understanding of the project vision and objectives with management will pay dividends. You make team member recommendations, but management makes the assignments.

On some projects your team may be selected without your input. That's fine as long as the level of experience and expertise of each SME is proportional to the difficulty, complexity, and centrality of their component.

Sometimes the assigned SMEs don't have the necessary experience and expertise. Maybe those that you would prefer for your team are working on different, higher priority projects. It is up to you to determine whether they are sufficient; whether they are feasible. If not, then be assertive in your request for more appropriate team members. Obviously not having the right people working with you greatly diminishes the probability of success. Maybe this isn't the right time to start the project. Maybe it would be better to wait until the right people are available. If you're told to "just make it work" maybe you don't have the management support you thought you had. Be sure to document your concerns.

Your Most Important Teammate

When leading a team, a large one in particular, it's important to have a trusted partner. Someone with whom you can speak freely and frankly behind closed doors, and who will speak equally freely and frankly with you. A partner with whom you share mutual respect.

I have repeatedly found that that the quality of Impossible Project deliverables is directly related to the quality of the working relationship between the lead and their partner.

This individual will probably be one of the SMEs on your team. Occasionally a project manager or agile release train engineer will assume this role, but it's usually easier to partner with a more technical peer. Regardless, they need to be able to align with you on the project vision and be expert enough to critically comment on your work products and contribute to your decision-making process.

Much has been written about the qualities that a leader should look for in a partner. When I was in college I took the Dale Carnegie Personalysis Test which measured strengths and weaknesses in organization, creativity, assertiveness, and interpersonal relationships. I remember being told at the time that if I entered into a business partnership that I should find someone that had strengths that complemented my weaknesses. More recently I took the Myers-Briggs test and received similar results and similar advice.

My experience differs slightly.

Communication, expertise, and trust are much more important than a check-the-box personality match.

It's not computer dating, although you are going to be working together very closely. You'll be addressing difficult issues and the conversations can get heated. Again, communication, expertise, and trust are key.

The movie *We Were Soldiers* portrays the Battle of Ia Drang, the first major American military engagement in the Vietnam War. Mel Gibson plays Lt. Col. Hal Moore and Sam Elliott plays his senior enlisted advisor, Sgt. Maj. Basil Plumley. Throughout the film, Plumley provides unwavering support to Moore. He also never holds back when offering his opinions and recommendations, informed by wisdom and experience. It is, at times, a difficult movie to watch, but Plumley's character is the model partner for your Impossible Project.

Embrace Your Ignorance

I once served as Lead Architect on a very large project where I had to produce process and data flow diagrams that included several application areas with which I was not familiar. Not surprisingly, they went through many, many iterations. After we had successfully delivered the project, the Domain Architect from one of those application areas approached me and said, "I knew when you were starting to understand [his domain area] because your drawings got less wrong."

I took it as the compliment he intended.

When you're leading a project, especially in a technical capacity, it's easy to feel like you have to know everything. After all, you're the one that everyone looks to for answers and it's easy to want to justify their confidence. It's not reasonable, though, to expect a single person to be an expert in all areas. The SMEs that you assemble for your team will know more about their domains than you do. A lot more. Lean into their expertise. Then go two steps farther:

Don't assume you know anything about anything.

Don't be afraid to be wrong.

Use your lack of familiarity as the perfect excuse to ask the "dumb" questions. Others are probably wondering the same thing, and you'll often notice looks of relief that you asked their questions.

Don't fool yourself into believing that something will make more sense later or that you'll figure it out eventually. Ask clarifying questions until you understand completely. Encourage your team to also ask clarifying questions until they understand completely.

Spend more time listening to others' solutions than talking about your own. Reflect your understanding back to them, and let them correct you.

Speaking of correcting you, the way you receive feedback, and the way that you're seen receiving feedback, is extraordinarily important to the team. It is a critical success factor. Really? Yes. Do more than encourage feedback. Go out of your way to solicit it, accept it, and embrace it. From everyone on the team. Never do anything to discourage it. One of the worst things that can happen to your project is to have people sitting at their desks with answers that they're afraid to give to you or questions that they're afraid to ask.

Many years ago, a mentor mentioned to me that some of the more junior team members were hesitant to meet with me because they thought I was intimidating. I had no idea. I didn't yell at anybody or offhandedly dismiss ideas or anything like that. If I were to make a list of adjectives to describe myself, intimidating would not come close to making the cut. I was told that it can sometimes be difficult for others to approach me simply because of my position within the organization and my role on the project. I suppose I can understand that. Even after twenty-five years my heart would still pound on my way to a meeting with a company executive. That's why it's important to not just be available but also to be encouraging and reach out.

Of course, nobody enjoys being corrected, having their worked critiqued, or their errors highlighted. You need to have a thick skin. Never lose sight of the fact that it's the end product that counts and don't take any of it personally. I understand that it's not easy. But it gets more tolerable the more you do it.

One approach that I often use is to emphasize to the team that the work product I'm asking them to review is far from its final form. It disarms them and invites more substantive participation. It signals that I really do value their thoughts, that I take them seriously, that I'm not going to be insulted by being corrected, and that I'm not going to scold them for giving the "wrong answer." Again, this can be difficult. It's our nature, especially as leaders, to want everything to be as perfect as possible before anyone else sees it. You may discover, perhaps paradoxically, that by distributing the less-finalized version your team will hold you in higher regard, morale will improve, and the product you all collectively produce will be better.

So, once your work product is past the dumpster heap of verbiage or spaghetti diagram stage, get others looking at it as quickly as possible. If you've opened the door to candid feedback and are encouraging fresh perspectives, the team will be comfortable sharing their thoughts with you and with each other. The faster you get something out, the faster you collect feedback, the more iterations you can cycle through, and the faster you'll improve the final product. And the more the team will learn along the way.

Finally, as leader, it is up to you to make the final decision about the changes that are made and that are not made. Deliberation cannot continue indefinitely. While you can't always incorporate everyone's feedback, you can always give it appropriate consideration.

Remedial Education

One very large project that I led required the integration of many different application areas. I was responsible for understanding how the data would find its way from one end of the company to the other, yet I had only the most basic idea about how most of these applications functioned.

So, at the beginning of the project I arranged for some key application area SMEs to present 45-minute overviews of their domains to the team. It didn't take much preparation on their part as most already had introductory materials at their fingertips.

I called it my "Remedial Education." Very early each morning for a week, a different SME presented their area to me and to anyone else in the group that chose to attend. I knew that those sessions would be helpful for me, and I figured that it would be useful for the team to get to know each other and their applications. I had no idea. The reception was tremendous; far beyond what I could have imagined.

Most everyone on the team attended most every day. That's rare for a week of morning meetings starting at 6:30 or 7:30, depending upon your time zone. The feedback was unanimously positive, and the sessions were so popular that a second week of "Remedial Education" was scheduled highlighting five more application areas.

Perhaps more importantly, during these two weeks the team members got to know each other well, giving them a level of comfort and cohesiveness that lasted throughout the project. Several people approached me after the product was delivered to say that these sessions were their favorite part of the project.

Brainstorming

If you want to learn more about brainstorming, seek out one of the myriad books, courses, videos, articles, and websites on the subject. At the point in your career where you are looking to lead an Impossible Project, you've probably held dozens of brainstorming and solutioning sessions. I do, though, want to share a couple of ideas that might help.

Capture the Conclusion, Not the Discussion

You've probably noticed that trust is one of the main themes of this book. It should therefore not come as a surprise when I mention the importance of trust when brainstorming. Open conversation and discussion are essential. Participants should feel safe exploring any idea regardless of how impractical or improbable it might seem at the time. That's the nature of brainstorming. And many times those seemingly off-the-wall suggestions either turn out to be right or stimulate thinking in the direction of a better solution.

Not having to tip-toe around potentially delicate challenges and issues accelerates solutioning. If challenges and issues exist, you need for them to be out in front of everyone so that they can be resolved. They're not going to go away on their own.

You might not know it at the time, but you may discover later that someone didn't raise a potential issue because they didn't feel safe or didn't feel like they'd be heard. While it is your responsibility to provide a supportive environment, it is your team members' responsibility to speak up, even when it's uncomfortable. Look at it this way: the team needs to be able to give and receive frank criticism in the afternoon, and then all go out to dinner together in the evening.

When it comes to published meeting minutes, I've seen far too many that read like a court transcript: "George suggested that it would be better to decrease the message size than to increase bandwidth. Tina disagreed, reminding the team that it is only using a fraction of the purchased bandwidth. Carl agreed with Tina, and Beth decided that the existing bandwidth would be sufficient to accommodate the larger messages."

No. Absolutely not.

Do not record or publish meeting minutes for brainstorming sessions. Capture only:

The list of participants

The key questions addressed and resolved

Some context for the decisions if appropriate (e.g. pros, cons, and rationale, but do not identify who advocated for each side)

Drawings, assumptions, and parking lot items

That's it.

Listen to the Whiteboard

When brainstorming, the whiteboard is the focal point of all of the expertise gathered in the room. And yes, brainstorming is much, much easier and much, much more effective when everyone is in the same room together. If you've ever been the one on the phone or video call while the rest of the team is in the conference room you know how hard it is to break in to say anything. Then, when you do get a word in you end up disrupting the whole conversational flow. Of course, that's if you can make out anything that's being said in the four overlapping conversations the first place. It's well worth the hit to the travel budget to bring everyone together for this exercise. Colocation also contributes to the cohesiveness of your core team, which will pay dividends that go far beyond travel cost as the project progresses.

As you're developing a solution, spend time listening to the whiteboard, either by yourself or with your team. "Listening to the whiteboard" is one of my favorite expressions and one of my favorite activities. I don't know why, but things look different when they're written in purple dry-erase marker. Draw some lines and boxes and arrows and squiggles and notes. Step back and take it in. Look. Think. Listen.

Let the whiteboard give you the answers.

I know it sounds a little bit crazy, but it will. Trust me. And trust it. The whiteboard will tell you if there's a problem. It will tell you what will work and what won't. It prevents you from projecting your own assumptions onto the solution. It allows you to more clearly see interrelationships.

But most importantly, drawing something on the board and explaining it to others (and to yourself) requires that you slow down, be explicit about the details, and really understand. After all, the best way to learn something is to teach it.

Priming the Brainstorming Pump

It's inevitable. At some point in your brainstorming session the ideas will slow to a trickle and then the well runs dry. Let's say the group has been working on ways to engage customers with a new product. Nobody's had anything new to contribute for a minute or two. The room has become quiet and maybe a little deflated.

One technique that I particularly like, and one that I have always found to be successful, is to spend some time brainstorming the opposite. In this example, instead of thinking about ways to engage customers with the new product, take ten minutes to come up with ways to repulse the customer with the new product.

This suggestion always gets a chuckle. Some may wonder if you're serious and really want them to spend time thinking about how to drive customers away. Some may be a little timid about sharing their ideas at first. But without fail the ideas start flowing and the energy goes back up. Way up. The team will get creative. Really, really creative. Maybe this activity taps into their own negative product experiences. Maybe it has something to do with our collective talent for complaining. At the end of the ten minutes you have accomplished three things. First, you have a great list of things to avoid. Second, you can probably add to the original list of ideas by considering the opposite of the items on the list of things to avoid. Third, when returning to the original exercise the team will almost always generate another burst of ideas.

One Hundred Questions

A variation on the general brainstorming exercise is to make a list of one hundred questions that need to be answered to deliver the project. They can be focused like, "Does the customer system capture email address?" or broad like, "How can we get information to the salesperson in the middle of the customer meeting?" You might already know many of the answers, but don't focus on that now. Answers come later.

I almost always make a list of one hundred questions myself for the projects that I lead. Sometimes I'll include others in the exercise, but rarely more than one or two, and most often just my partner.

The first couple dozen come easily, and then the wall. The whole point is to push past the obvious to reach the "second level." This is where you're thinking most creatively, uncovering the more critical and oftentimes unexpected questions. These are the ones that would otherwise come as a surprise later in the project. Better to get them on the table early. More often than not, once I get this second wind, I'll blow past one hundred, exceeding it by thirty or fifty or more.

Putting it All Together

It's still early in the project and you have a tremendous amount of great information. You have a Big Box Diagram. You have ideas from one or more brainstorming sessions. You have a long list of questions. But all this information is only useful if it informs the project structure and the team's subsequent activities.

No doubt you're continuing to refine the Big Box Diagram as you learn more about the solution components. In the first weeks and months the project expect it to change drastically and frequently. You might not know all of the details about all of the systems or applications yet, but you're getting closer. You will see the solution starting to take shape in some areas. Others will need more attention.

At this point you can start answering the one hundred questions. Many will directly inform the Big Box Diagram, team composition, and/or project direction. You may only be able to answer a few, with the remainder requiring additional thought, research, and discussion. After all, you started with at least a hundred. In the next chapter I'll introduce the use of Issue Trackers for capturing and assigning questions and concerns. We'll also talk about the importance of identifying and resolving the most perplexing questions first.

Manage the Overwhelmingness

An Impossible Project is inherently overwhelming. It's easy to become stressed, especially when you're leading. So many moving parts. Nothing seems to go together. And you have to update management with the team's progress by the end of the week.

It'll happen. Expect it.

You have your Big Box Diagram so you know how the whole thing fits together. You have the overall context. The key, then, is to continually decompose your Impossible Project into smaller and smaller pieces, dividing-and-conquering until each becomes manageable itself. Until each piece becomes "feasible."

Also, remember that you are not responsible for the details of each individual piece. Sometimes it's hard to let go. You want to go deep into all the details. You probably enjoy the details and at minimum you're interested. But there's only so much time and only so much attention and only so much energy, and yours is better spent elsewhere. That's why you have an entire team working with you and for you.

Oftentimes when I'm feeling scattered I'll create a Mind Map to help organize my thoughts. If you're not already using Mind Maps, I would very strongly encourage you to look into them. Free and not-very-expensive software, along with how-to websites, books, and videos are readily available.

A *Mind Map* visually and spatially organizes information, ideas, and concepts. It starts with a central topic or main idea. Related words, phrases, categories, ideas, and even images branch hierarchically from that central topic. This can be helpful when breaking down a large concept into more manageable chunks.

You may discover that a project plan or work breakdown structure will emerge from the Mind Map. It may lead you step-by-step through the thought process which leads to the solution to a vexing problem. Listening to the Mind Map and following the trail of ideas wherever it leads is just like listening to the whiteboard. Sometimes you don't know where you'll end up until you start.

An Example Mind Map

You spent some time brainstorming the grocery store curbside pickup project with your team and generated a lot of notes. Here's a Mind Map that organizes some of that information.

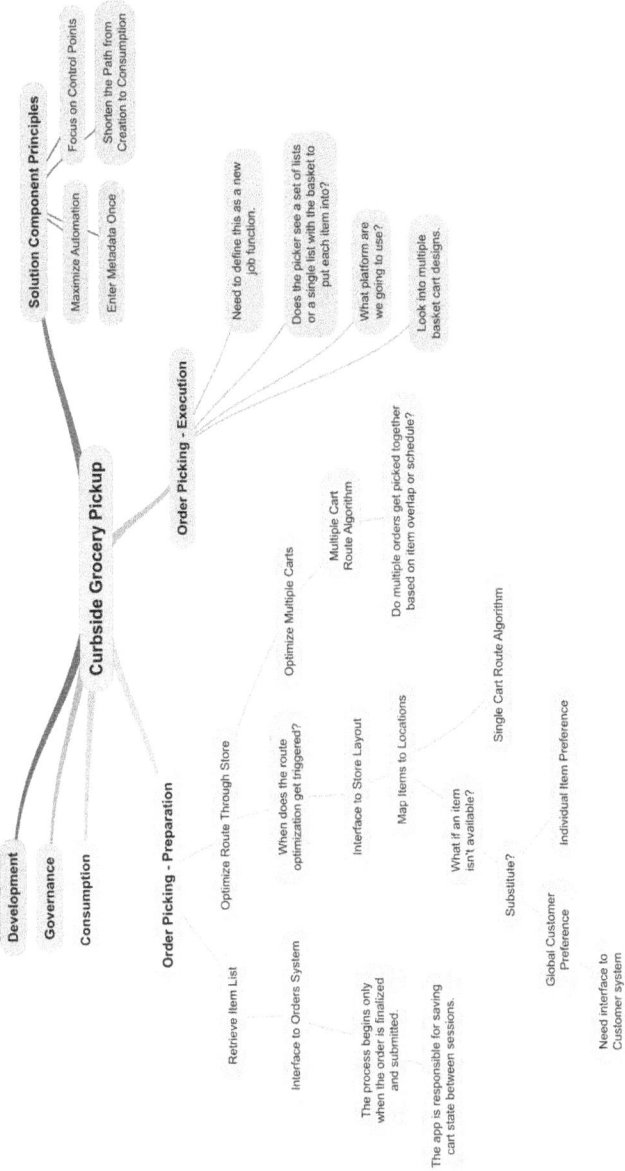

Curbside Grocery Pickup

Development

Governance

Consumption

Solution Component Principles

- Maximize Automation
- Enter Metadata Once
- Focus on Control Points
- Shorten the Path from Creation to Consumption

Order Picking - Execution

- Need to define this as a new job function.
- Does the picker see a set of lists or a single list with the basket to put each item into?
- What platform are we going to use?
- Look into multiple basket cart designs.

Order Picking - Preparation

- Retrieve Item List
  - Interface to Orders System
  - The process begins only when the order is finalized and submitted.
  - The app is responsible for saving cart state between sessions.
- Optimize Route Through Store
  - When does the route optimization get triggered?
  - Optimize Multiple Carts
    - Multiple Cart Route Algorithm
    - Do multiple orders get picked together based on item overlap or schedule?
  - Interface to Store Layout
    - Map Items to Locations
    - Single Cart Route Algorithm
  - What if an item isn't available?
    - Substitute?
      - Global Customer Preference
      - Individual Item Preference
    - Need interface to Customer system

General areas for consideration were placed off to the side in the upper-left corner. Not sure what we're going to do with those, but we don't want to lose the thoughts.

The team also discussed general Solution Component Principles. Those are in the upper-right. They thought it would be useful to have some guidelines to help inform the design. They don't think the list is complete yet, but it seemed like a good start.

Of course, the Mind Map for a project of this size would be significantly larger. Only the Order Picking Preparation and Execution branches are included here.

Notice that the team was pretty clear about what needed to be done to implement Preparation. A few outstanding questions, but a work breakdown is starting to emerge. Not so much about Execution. It appears that this is a brand new function for the company and fulfillment doesn't appear to have been worked through.

If you choose to capture project details in a Mind Map, expect it to evolve. Just like your Big Box Diagram it will become more detailed and more correct as the solution comes into focus.

Set the Tone For Your Team

Following the delivery of one especially Impossible Project a friend me pulled me aside. He said that he appreciated that I never wavered in my direction for the project and in my confidence in the team, even when the mood got dark and many doubted whether we would succeed. He said that he internalized that confidence and then projected it to his own workgroup. That meant a lot to me.

Your team will reflect the tone that you set.

You are its North Star. Be a steadying influence, even when everyone else is struggling with uncertainty and doubt. Acknowledge their concerns then reorient their attention toward a solution.

Ensure that everyone on your team feels valued, respected, and appreciated. Encourage open communication. Be a good listener. When arbitrating disputes, be attentive to all of the arguments, then make a decision and move forward. In the best case, endless debate leads to unnecessary churn, and in the worst case it leads to the entrenchment of competing positions.

You may end up on the losing side of an argument yourself. It happens to everyone. You may be certain that the approach advocated by someone else is completely brain-dead and will lead to unnecessary problems later. You may even be proven right in the end. But if when you escalate the issue and make your case the decision is not in your favor, lick your wounds and make that alternative approach work anyway.

Be intentional about how you want members of your team to interact with each other. You will always get more of the good behaviors you demonstrate and more of the bad behaviors you tolerate. Verbalize your expectation that the team be supportive and collaborative and never mistrustful, passive-aggressive, or secretive. This, of course, applies to you, too.

Finally, and perhaps most importantly, care for and about those you're leading. Authentically. You can't fake it. And if you can't do it, you may be wise to consider a different role. Be aware of the emotional health of your team members. A group can be pushed very, very hard. They will deliver. But there will be consequences. I already mentioned the development group that quit immediately after completing a Death March project, leaving no one to support their deliverable. On the other hand, recognizing that a team member needs a night off and a night out with their spouse at the company's expense can do wonders for morale and, as experience suggests, will still be remembered decades later.

Fourth Secret: Revealed

Cast a Wide Net

- Do not try to be both lead and subject matter expert.

- Always have a working understanding of the project, illustrated using a Big Box Diagram.

- Break the project down into smaller and smaller pieces until each individual piece is feasible.

- Don't assume that you know anything about anything.

- Involve everyone you believe may be impacted by the project at the outset, then pare down the team as the solution comes into focus.

- Identify a trusted partner.

- Provide opportunities for team members to share a baseline understanding of their areas with each other.

- Brainstorm in person.

- Be a steadying influence and an example of the comportment you want from your team.

- Care for and about your team members.

Fifth Secret

Identify and Answer the Key Questions First

As you and your team brainstorm, you will undoubtedly discover questions, unknowns, and assumptions that you know will be central to solving the problem. They could be technical, business process, organizational, or political. Information needs to get from one system to another but no interface exists between them. Workflows designed and implemented a certain way need to function differently. A new capability must be developed from scratch. A pivotal group is not participating.

Those questions, unknowns, and assumptions must become your obsession as soon as they are discovered. Drive their prioritization and resolution. After all, you are synthesizing the information from your subject matter experts (SMEs) into a cross-functional solution. You understand how the pieces fit together. You have the broadest perspective. You have visibility into how a problem in one area impacts others.

If you find that you cannot resolve an issue on your own or with your team, find additional SMEs from the impacted areas and ask questions. You may find that you overlooked a domain area when building your team. You may need to seek advice from outside consultants.

Oftentimes when the hard problems are solved, other pieces fall into place. The easy problems may no longer be a concern or they may go away on their own. Don't spend time on the minutiae when big issues remain.

It doesn't matter if you resolve every other problem if the key questions remain.

One large unknown can ripple uncertainty throughout the project, and if you guess wrong, time spent on these smaller issues may end up being wasted. And on an Impossible Project you definitely don't have time to waste.

Never assume that a big problem will resolve itself or go away on its own. It won't. A miracle will not occur.

"Maybe you could be a bit more explicit at step three."

Key questions come in two types: barriers to finding a Feasible Solution and roadblocks that impede progress toward any solution. The former are typically technical in nature, and are usually discovered early in the project. The latter are typically political or organizational, and can arise at any time.

Once issues are identified they must be tracked and managed. I'll cover that in this chapter as well.

Barriers to a Feasible Solution

These challenges should consume your focus. After all, if they cannot be resolved, then the project or feature must be reconsidered. There's no point in spending time on a solution that will have to be fundamentally reframed or scrapped. Their most common form is a seemingly uncrossable process chasm.

In one very early project, the key question was how to get a message from one system to another. Seems straightforward. But not only did the systems not communicate with each other, they used incompatible technologies where no messaging interface existed at all. As with any chasm, you can either build a bridge across it or find a path around it. We ended up finding a path around it. It wasn't elegant, but it got the job done. And at that point we were happy to find any solution at all, no matter how barely feasible.

Roadblocks to Any Solution

The second set of challenges are those that impede progress toward any solution. They are typically political and organizational, usually involve resource allocation, and must be resolved by management. These are the types of problems that can quickly transform an Impossible Project into a Death March. They can also take a long time to resolve.

Engage with management as soon as the issue becomes apparent so that they can start working on it. You can help by articulating the need, identifying pros and cons, and projecting the consequences of inaction.

One of the hardest things to do in any company is something that's not already being done; unless, of course, there's funding or incremental headcount attached to it. When a project requires the implementation of a new capability, somebody needs to do it. You may have no takers for a long time. Ultimately, the impasse will be broken by an upper management volunteer (or voluntold). Progress can still be made in other areas while this gets worked out, but such a problem can become a fatal showstopper if it remains unresolved.

The Metro Diagram

It's pretty obvious to see how you can contribute to overcoming barriers to a Feasible Solution, but you can have just as significant an impact clearing roadblocks.

A group I was working with believed that the project would require unusually extensive testing across a multitude of different data pathways. We were having trouble getting enough testers assigned to the project. We were told that we had enough for any required point-to-point testing.

I tried unsuccessfully to communicate that there was no such thing as point-to-point testing on that project.

Instead, the testing would need to be point-to-point-to-point-to-point-to-point.

The diagram illustrating that point may have been the most impactful I ever made. Using the Washington, DC Metro map as inspiration, I represented each data pathway as a subway line. Large circles were junctions where multiple processes intersected. Small dots were stations implementing individual process steps along the way.

That approach is not unique. I've seen many others use the same metaphor to make similar points. The illustration below is not the actual diagram, but a fictitious example.

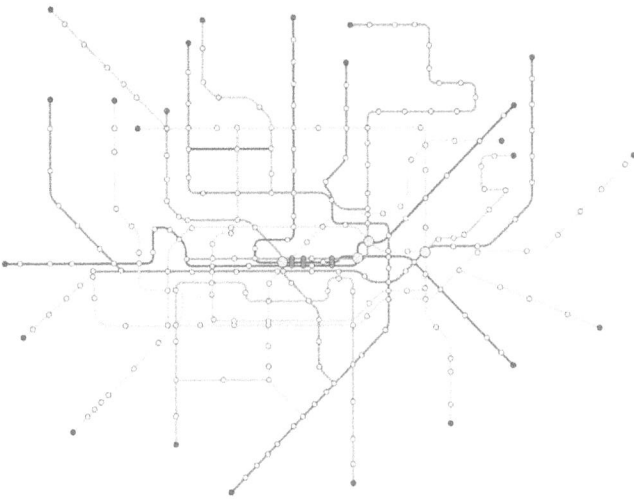

Metro Diagram

The interconnectedness of the processes became immediately apparent to everyone, and the appropriate resources were allocated. In this case, a picture truly was worth a thousand words, and emails and meetings and hall conversations and phone calls.

Issue Tracking

Every large, complex project will require processes and infrastructure to organize and manage its assets. These include source code, documentation, and metadata repositories, monitoring, logging, defect tracking, deployment infrastructure, testing and quality analysis tools, project management, and issue tracking.

I love Issue Trackers.

> **Next to your trusted partner, your issue tracking system is your best friend.**

Record every question, problem, idea, and roadblock that cannot be resolved immediately. This is especially true at the beginning of the project when you're putting together your Big Box Diagram and brainstorming with your team.

Quick Note: Issue Trackers are not for capturing bugs, incidents, problems, or errors. Those are handled by one or more other ticketing systems. Don't mix them up.

Beyond that, though, capture everything. Don't assume that anyone will remember anything. It doesn't matter if you have a photographic memory and can keep the details of hundreds of issues straight in your head. I know that I can't. It's easy to lose track of which questions have already been answered and which issues have already been resolved. Besides, the rest of your team needs access to those details, too. Over time, Issue Trackers will contain some of the most valuable project documentation.

We've all been in meetings where we have the same

conversation about the same issue with the same people over and over again. You don't want that to happen on your project. Create an Issue Tracker. Assign it. Move on.

Issue Tracking Software

It's possible to capture issues using simple lists in Microsoft Word or Excel if that's your only option. It's better than nothing, but it wouldn't be my preferred approach. At the other end of the sophistication scale are integrated project management, and application development and deployment environments. Some newer packages even incorporate artificial intelligence to identify similar issues, automatically generate descriptive tags, and assign resolution responsibility.

For the purpose of this discussion, let's assume that we are using an issue management system with basic capabilities and minimum automation that captures the following details:

Short Title

Description

Dependencies

Team Member Who Opened the Issue Tracker

Priority: Low, Medium, High, and Critical

Status: Open, Deferred, Closed - Resolved, Closed - Cancelled, Pending Review

Required Resolution Date

Team Member Assigned

The Lifecycle of an Issue Tracker

Issue Tracker creation and curation process details vary from company to company and even project to project. Many leads and project managers have their own preferences, and your project management software may dictate some of the process. Regardless, the lifecycle of an Issue Tracker will generally have four steps: creation, assignment, resolution, validation, and closing.

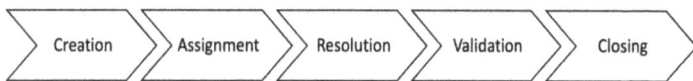

> Creation   >> Assignment   >> Resolution   >> Validation   >> Closing

Issue Tracker Lifecycle

Creation: Anyone should be able to create or contribute to an Issue Tracker, from the Summer Intern to the Officer-in-Charge. I believe that it is better to err on the side of too many Issue Trackers than run the risk of overlooking a potential problem by limiting them. Besides, many modern project management platforms will identify, flag, and deduplicate similar entries. Enter the details: title, description, etc. Capture as much descriptive information as possible, especially whether its resolution depends upon another issue or deliverable. The initial priority is assigned by the person that opens the Issue Tracker, based upon the urgency with which they believe the issue needs to be resolved. Later, the project manager, lead, or management can adjust the priority, although the requester usually knows best. General questions or observations are given Low priority while errors that prevent progress or produce failure conditions are probably High or Critical.

Assignment: Before submitting the Issue Tracker, the requester assigns it to the team member believed to be best equipped to resolve it. Keep in mind that this initial assignment is often only a guess. Inevitably, someone will get an Issue Tracker that doesn't seem to have anything to do with their area of expertise. I've had team members approach me concerned that they were assigned an Issue Tracker that they had no idea how to resolve. It's not a problem. Just have it forwarded to you or to the project manager. An Issue Tracker may move from team member to team member as each contributes a portion of the solution. Some teams prefer to assign all Issue Trackers to the project manager first. That certainly reduces the likelihood of an issue being bounced around like a hot potato. On the other hand, the project manager can become a bottleneck and slow down the process.

Resolution: Add details to the Description as the issue is researched and resolved. Capture the thought process so that it can be referenced rather than reconstructed later. Update the Issue Tracker periodically according to its priority. Critical and High daily. Medium and Low as events warrant. While researching and resolving an issue you may identify additional dependencies, prerequisites, or unknowns. In that case it's better to open new Issue Trackers and capture the dependencies than it is to overload a single one.

Validation and Closing: It is the responsibility of the person who opened the Issue Tracker to close it when they are satisfied with the resolution. Set the Issue Tracker status to Pending Review and reassign it to the requester. If your issue tracking software doesn't have a Pending Review status, you can co-opt an infrequently used priority or status for that purpose. Some teams require additional sign-off by the project manager. You may want to approve as well; however, you will probably be involved in the resolution itself and don't need the additional paperwork step. Besides, you should maintain awareness anyway.

Managing Issue Trackers

It doesn't do any good to capture issues if they are not reviewed, resolved, and referenced. You won't necessarily be the one to manage the Issue Trackers. That task typically falls to the project manager. Nevertheless, you should take a daily active interest in anything that's Critical or High priority.

At every project status meeting, either you or the project manager should review each open Critical and High priority Issue Tracker, as well as those that have been recently closed. Medium priority issues do not have to be discussed as often; perhaps once a month to run through the full list to make sure they are still relevant.

Very important procedural point: the purpose for these Issue Tracker reviews is to get their status. It is not to discuss or resolve them.

One of the best project managers I ever worked with would step through the Critical and High priority Issue Trackers each week and ask the team member to whom it was assigned for an update. No commentary. No conversation. And if any arose it would be cut off. Maybe five or ten seconds for most issues. Then move on to the next one. A minute was considered an overly-long discussion. She was specifically interested in the following questions:

> Has the issue been resolved? If so, what was the resolution? Briefly!! Next.

> Otherwise, when will the issue be resolved?

> Is the issue on track to be resolved by the due date?

> If no due date has been set, what outstanding questions or problems need to be addressed first, and when will those be resolved?

> Is the Issue Tracker being updated appropriately in terms of content and frequency?

> Do you need anything from the group? If so, what do you need and from whom?

> Do you need a follow-up conversations? If so, what do you need to discuss and with whom?

The meetings moved along very efficiently, and nobody wanted to be the one that had to say in front of the group that they hadn't made any progress.

—

You're not going to fully resolve every Issue Tracker, just like you're not going to fully resolve every defect. Certainly those that are Critical and High, and probably most that are Medium. As the project approaches its conclusion, be intentional about which issues need to be resolved and which do not. At least not now. The latter can become features for future versions.

Fifth Secret: Revealed

Identify and Answer the Key Questions First

- It doesn't do any good to resolve small questions when large questions remain outstanding.

- Anything that is an impediment to developing a Feasible Solution should be your overwhelming focus.

- Capture all outstanding questions, problems, and ideas in Issue Trackers.

- Leverage Issue Tracking software.

- Collect Issue Tracker status–no discussion, only status–as part of the regular project status meeting.

- Issue Trackers contain some of the most valuable project documentation and should be curated and managed accordingly.

Sixth Secret

Communicate Honestly and Build Trust

The successful leadership of an Impossible Project is built upon a foundation of trust:

Trust that management has in you to guide your team.

Trust that you have in management to support you and your team.

Trust that your team has in you to hear them, advocate for them, and collaboratively formulate a solution with them.

Trust that you have in your team to be forthright and to work to the best of their ability to deliver the project.

The worst thing that you can do on any project, not just an Impossible Project, is to erode trust. It's easy to do, and you'll have no shortage of opportunities. Once damaged, it is extraordinarily difficult to repair.

Creative Writing and Strategic Obfuscation

It's happened to all of us. Probably many times. A program just doesn't want to work right. The data doesn't contain what you thought it would. An assumption turned out to be incorrect. The nature of an Impossible Project guarantees that this is going to happen.

Nobody wants to be the bearer of bad news, especially to their boss or customer. Nobody wants to delay someone else's work or be a risk in the critical path. And that's when we draw upon our creative writing skills.

We frame the problem in the least negative way possible. We obscure the truth behind a tsunami of positive-sounding verbiage that appears to say that everything is progressing within acceptable parameters and that the team is focused to the best of its ability and beyond to produce the required deliverables on time and under budget subject to the expected headwinds that are typical for such a project. Like that. With ranch dressing on that word salad. The hope is that nobody actually perseveres to the end of the sentence and asks what the typical, expected headwinds are for such a project.

We hide our delays when someone else's are the focus, sitting silently allowing them to take the blame for pushing back a deliverable date when in reality we're not ready either.

We speak optimistically about finding a solution even when we have no idea how or when we're going to find it. We buy time, hoping for inspiration or divine intervention so that the problem is resolved by the next time we're asked. Sometimes we get lucky. Most of the times we don't. And now we've got a bigger problem.

The most uncomfortable questions you can face in any work setting begin with "Why did you…? and "Why didn't you …?"

Why didn't you ask for help when you were having trouble with the program? Why didn't you create an Issue Tracker when the data didn't look right? Why did you wait so long for that other group to reply before notifying me?

You know what they say about tangled webs. Eventually you can't cover up or obfuscate or talk your way out any longer. You're forced to come clean and answer all those "Why did or didn't you...?" questions. These meetings are never pleasant.

You have also created a trust problem for yourself. Whoever is asking these questions now believes that they must keep a close eye on you. They get all up in your business because they don't have confidence that you will communicate accurately with them. They wonder what you aren't telling them. You never want to be on someone's mind in that way, and it's a mindset that's very hard to rehabilitate.

A friend once told me that he keeps the "Why did you...?" and "Why didn't you...?" questions at the front of his mind whenever he has a decision to make. The actions he takes, or chooses not to take, are informed by that future conversation with his boss. Having good answers to those questions is a positive indication that the decision has been well considered. Having poor answers, or none at all, suggests that the decision still requires some more thought.

Honest Reporting Always

You can expect an Impossible Project to have more than its share of problems, delays, unknowns, and things that just don't go as planned. But then again, that's what makes an Impossible Project interesting. When the unexpected happens, you will be called upon to explain the what, why, how, who, and when.

The best way to build trust with your management, customers, and team is to simply be honest. I know. Simple but not always easy.

Be scrupulously honest, especially in your status reports and updates. All stakeholders need to be confident that you will always be up front with them. That they will always know exactly what's happening. After all, they answer to their own customers, stakeholders, and management.

Highlight threats to success and items that require leadership action and involvement. Document challenges and problems, as well as proposed solutions.

If something isn't going as expected, say that. Invoke the Quality Triangle: resources, time, scope, and quality. Be dispassionate about any adjustments that may be necessary, as well as the consequences of not making them. Be clear about the support you need from your stakeholders and from management. You might not always get what you ask for, and that may necessitate additional adjustments.

Keeping complete and accurate status information will pay dividends later in the project. At some point you will invariably be asked why some activity took longer than expected or why some adjustment was made. If you've kept all the details you can easily and authoritatively answer those questions.

Having said all that, as with everything in life, there is a balance. Being overly nervous or CYA can erode leadership's confidence in you to handle challenges. Think about the communication you would want to see from others on your team, and let that guide your communication to your leadership.

Setting Timelines

Timelines are always a touchy subject and frequently a source of friction between your management, your customers, your team, and you.

It is axiomatic that any project will take 110% of the time allocated to it, so you need to find a balance between jeopardizing quality by being unreasonably aggressive, and unnecessarily delaying product release by being excessively cautious. Most everyone works better under a deadline and a little urgency.

Final release dates are often tied to major events having long lead times and little or no flexibility. These include conferences, public corporate events, Super Bowl advertisements, multi-channel marketing campaigns, etc.

You'll know you're on track, or not, by your progress through the intermediate milestones, especially those addressing the previously discussed key questions.

I prefer to set very aggressive deadlines at the outset. The first response from the team is usually, "Are you kidding?" or something maybe a little less polite.

So, I ask them how much time they'll need; for the dates that they prefer and are comfortable committing to. Take your cues from the team. I get a lot of insight into the feasibility of the project as a whole from this exercise.

I use their dates if at all possible and advocate for their timeline. It's another way that to demonstrate that I am listening to them and that I value their input. More often than not they will be reasonable, and reasonably accurate. They also tend to be more aggressive than the "reasonable" dates I would have proposed. But perhaps most importantly, the team will take more accountability for their dates than for mine (or for someone else's).

Build Trust and Demand Honesty

By keeping your status updates complete, accurate, and dispassionate, it will be clear to your team that you are never looking to undermine anyone or to cover anything up. The status is always just what it is. Favoritism, regardless of whether it is real or perceived, undermines trust. "Why" questions from your team like, "Why did you gloss over that other group's issue while highlighting mine?" can be just as uncomfortable as those from management.

Demonstrate to your team, through your actions more than your words, that you hear them and that you advocate on their behalf. Focus on the "we" instead of the "I."

Some issues are more difficult to resolve than others, and being "on the list" week after week can become demoralizing. Provide or arrange for the help your team needs. Nobody gets everything they want, but you must be sincere in your efforts.

At the same time, demand honesty from your team in their assessments of your work products and in their own progress. Stress to them that neither you nor management can help if they don't communicate. Just like you don't want management to be all up in your business, don't be all up in theirs.

Make Friends with Red

Project progress and confidence levels are often expressed with traffic signal colors and shapes like green circles, yellow triangles, and red stop signs. Accessibility tip: use both colors and shapes. You'd be surprised by the number of color blind people you work with. Plus, it's helpful when you print the status report on a black-and-white printer.

On Track

At Risk

Off Track

Not Started

Complete

Dropped

In general, green means that the project is progressing according to plan with high confidence. Yellow indicates some issue requires awareness, and that while the project plan has not necessarily been impacted yet, it will be without intervention. Red draws immediate attention to a deadline that has been missed or for which there is low confidence. Corrective action and a recovery plan are required. Some project managers extend this system to include gray squares for tasks that have not yet started, blue stars for those that are complete, and black diamonds for dropped or de-scoped items.

Too often management, project managers, and maybe even you as lead become hyper-focused on anything with a red status, ignoring or taking for granted all other progress. We've all had managers who seem to see red whenever they see red, demanding explanations and dispensing beatings.

This approach jeopardizes the project and undermines trust. It may also be an indication that your Impossible Project is becoming a Death March. The consequences of the failure to address this mindset, either in yourself or in other leadership, are devastating. Future status reports will surely show more green and yellow, and progress will appear to be improving. But these reports will also contain a whole lot more creative writing and a whole lot less of the critical information that leadership needs.

Good executive sponsors, managers, leads, project managers, and customers recognize that the unexpected and the temporarily unexplainable will happen. They should already know it, but it doesn't hurt to reiterate it.

One of the greatest contributions that management can make to an Impossible Project is to give it the "freedom to be red."

Many of the task and milestone statuses in an Impossible Project will be red much of the time, and whenever there's a red status on the page you will invariably be asked why. Probably by several different stakeholders. Your first priority is understanding the problem. Immediately.

Then, lay out a plan for getting it back to green.

While nobody wants to see a red status, your Impossible Project will be OK as long as there's always a plan.

Trust me. I once led a very large Impossible Project that was in overall red status for a whole host of different reasons throughout almost its entire lifespan. The only tongue-lashings I ever received were when I didn't have a remediation plan. Sometimes the problem didn't have an obvious solution and sometimes I didn't know how exactly we were going to fix it, but I always had to have a plan or a series of steps or questions or action items that would move us in the right direction.

Lean into Feasible → Preferable → Optimal. What has to be true to make it work? Are there prerequisite steps? Call in the impacted subject matter experts and brainstorm. Create a plan, then work it step by step. Always keep asking questions and always keep moving forward.

Help One Another

Very early in my career a supervisor told me that once I've spent an hour on a problem, stop, pick up the phone, and call somebody for help. The phone call instruction gives you an idea of the timeframe, but the message still applies. In fact, today one shouldn't need to struggle for nearly that long. We have so many more resources: website searches, instant messaging, online knowledge bases, and even AI.

Be quick to ask for help and generous in providing help.

This runs counter to many corporate cultures that value self-reliance and empire building over efficient problem solving and resource leveraging. Asking questions is too often seen as a lack of skill or expertise, and answering questions is too often seen as a distraction.

Get over it.

Now.

This is an Impossible Project.

There's no time for that foolishness.

An Impossible Project requires the best solutions, wherever they come from, as quickly as possible. Encourage … no, demand that everyone on the team ask questions and contribute answers. It simply becomes part of the daily routine.

As lead, though, you have a peculiar superpower:

You have the ability to shut down a conversation by simply commenting.

You might not want that to happen, but it will. If you weigh in too quickly, over time you will increasingly be looked to for "the answer," even though you might not be the the best one to give it. Your team will wait for you even when they should be asserting themselves. Yes, questions need to be answered quickly, but solicit and hear others' thoughts first. Be comfortable with the silence while waiting for others to speak.

Assume Positive Intent

Honesty, frankness, and directness. Yes, yes, and yes. But above all, respect. Do not tolerate incivility. The project is impossible enough already without being undermined from within.

Encourage spirited debate, especially when working through the most difficult key questions, but team members must always be respectful. Keep the focus of the arguments on the issues and solutions. First ground rule: never make it personal.

The best way I've found to keep these discussions productive is through a second simple ground rule: assume positive intent. The idea is to presuppose that the person with whom you're speaking has good intentions despite seemingly harmful words or actions. Give them the benefit of the doubt and assume that their top priority is the same as yours: to solve the problem. Refrain from reflexively jumping to negative conclusions about their motives.

Now, assuming positive intent does not mean pollyannaishly ignoring hostility. Sometimes a team member really is malicious and may need to be coached or replaced for the good of the team. But you'll be amazed at how much the filter through which you interpret input affects your response, mindset, and even your mood. When you assume positive intent you are better able to hear what's being said, processing it more effectively and less defensively.

Expect and Manage Doubt

My experience is that in every large project there comes a point where doubt creeps in. Is the project really possible? I mean, it's an Impossible Project, but is it really not possible? Can it be delivered at least reasonably close to the target date? Did we bite off more than we can chew? Is this going to derail my career? Am I going to get fired when management abandons the project? They can become all-consuming and paralyzing.

This phenomenon is often referred to as a mid-project slump or mid-project plateau. I find that this happens at about a third to half-way through the project. You're past the initial excitement and honeymoon period. You and your team have invested significant effort, but cannot yet see the light at the end of the tunnel. You've uncovered most of the key issues, but many, perhaps most, have not yet been resolved.

It's natural to experience this kind of trough, wondering whether the project will be successful. And even if it is successful, will it be worth it? Frustration, stagnation, and doubt are all normal. Expect it in your team and expect it in yourself.

Lean into your partner and encourage them to lean into you. Provide mutual support to each other, and do not allow yourselves to get sucked into a downward spiral of self-reinforcing despair. It's also important to work everything out behind closed doors. Both of you. Do not allow your concerns to contaminate your team. They will take their cues from you. The trust that you've built up with your team will now pay its greatest dividends.

Dissertation Doldrums

I started my dissertation research in earnest in the fall, but by the following summer the methodology I had proposed still wasn't working. I tried many, many different approaches and succeeded only in eliminating them as possibilities. I could even explain why most had failed, but it seemed that anything resembling progress only led to more dead ends.

I started to become concerned to the point of near-panic that I would have to abandon the topic and start all over again. Doubts about the usefulness of the research crept in.

Fortunately, I made a breakthrough in the late summer, refined what turned out to be a successful methodology, explored several use cases, and received my degree.

Many years later, a friend who was about half-way through her Ph.D. program and experiencing some challenges with her research asked whether it was normal to wonder whether it was all worth it. I told her that I had experienced exactly the same worries and doubts at exactly the same point in the process.

I got curious so I asked that question to everybody I knew that had entered a Ph.D. program. The response was unanimous. Every single person had wrestled with those same worries and doubts. Some decided that the cost of continuing was greater than the benefit and left. Others continued with varying amounts of frustration and success. It is clear that in any substantive endeavor, these feelings are normal, and should be expected.

When confronting these feelings with your team, first acknowledge that they exist and that they are normal. That said, the team must then be reoriented forward, both toward near-term and long-term objectives. Focus them on the next deliverable and what they should be doing right now. The "next play." Remind them of the benefits that justified the project's existence in the first place. It's easy to lose sight of the big picture, especially when you're nose-down in the details. Rekindle some of the excitement that the team had at the very beginning.

Other suggestions for overcoming a mid-project slump include:

Simplifying tasks into smaller chunks that can be completed more quickly to build momentum.

Celebrating small wins to boost morale.

Encouraging short breaks to avoid burnout (see the *Silent Night* sidebar in the First Secret).

Providing additional resources if available and useful.

Engaging in team-building activities to encourage cohesiveness.

Next Play

In his book Beyond Basketball: Coach K's Keywords for Success,* *Mike Krzyzewski describes his "Next Play" philosophy:*

> *"In basketball and in life, I have always maintained the philosophy of 'next play.' Essentially, what it means is that what you have just done is not nearly as important as what you are doing right now. The 'next play' philosophy emphasizes the fact that the most important play of the game or life moment on which you should always focus is the next one. It is not about the turnover I committed last time down the court, it's not even about the three-pointer I hit to tie the game, it is about what's next.*

> *"To waste time lamenting a mistake or celebrating success is distracting and can leave you and your team unprepared for what you are about to face. It robs you of the ability to do your best at that moment and to give your full concentration. It's why I love basketball. Plays happen with rapidity and there may be no stop-action. Basketball is a game that favors the quick thinker and the person who can go on to the next play fastest."*

Leading an Impossible Project also requires forward focus and favors the quick thinker. Concentrate on your next play. Don't ruminate on the past. Problems, challenges, and issues are constant companions. Resolve them. Move on.

---

* Krzyzewski, Mike. *Beyond Basketball: Coach K's Keywords for Success.* New York: Business Plus, 2006.

Beware of management that demands that you not even acknowledge the existence of any negative feelings by your team. Pretending that they don't exist is an overt rejection of their concerns. It is disingenuous, counterproductive, and damaging to the team and to the project. An Impossible Project can turn into a Death March that fast. If you are stuck with this kind of management, shield your team and protect yourself from them as much as possible.

Finally, back in the Second Secret I talked about the impact of uncertainty and change. When the team is wrestling with doubt, make scope change your last resort. It's too easy for that to become a crutch. The problem may not be ability to deliver, but rather fatigue and maybe a little frustration.

Stay the course whenever possible.

—

There. You now have the tools to maximize the likelihood that you will successfully deliver your next Impossible Project. But I still have one more Secret to share.

Sixth Secret: Revealed

Communicate Honestly and Build Trust

- Always be complete, accurate, and honest in your status reports and updates. Always.

- Document everything.

- Advocate on behalf of the team with management. Be honest and demand honesty.

- Expect status reports with roadblocks, delays, and reduced confidence. Prepare management for them.

- If all your management cares about is "getting the red out," demanding explanations and dispensing beatings, your Impossible Project may become a Death March. Address this concern with them immediately.

- Whenever you report a red status, have a plan for getting it back on track, or at least a plan for identifying the prerequisite activities.

- Create an environment where everyone on the team is comfortable asking for help.

- Ensure that everyone allocates time to answer teammates' questions.

- Give your team an opportunity to comment and discuss before you wade into the conversation and inadvertently shut it down.

- Scope change is a last resort when the team is wrestling with doubt.

Bonus Secret

Transition Leadership When the Project is Delivered

You've found a trusted partner, assembled your team of experts, and laid out a solution through multiple Big Box Diagram iterations. The key questions have been identified and are being resolved. Each subject matter expert is empowered to solve problems within their own domain, and you are addressing issues that arise between domains. You've discovered the places where you guessed right and the places where you had to try again. You have at least a Feasible Solution and are working toward a Preferable Solution. The team is executing the plan and the project is moving forward on its own momentum. You've even made it through the mid-project slump.

Maybe you can see the light at the end of the tunnel. Or maybe not yet. The project may still seem impossible. Questions about its feasibility may remain right up until the time of delivery.

By this point, though, your most significant contributions to the project are likely behind you.

The nature of your involvement will change as the project transitions from design, architecture, and planning to development, testing, and delivery. It doesn't matter whether the team is using a waterfall or agile methodology. I've always considered my job as leader of an Impossible Project well done if my day-to-day involvement diminishes over time. When placed on the right path and working the plan, the team will know what to do. The best thing that I can do is to get out of their way. Eventually, most of my time is spent answering questions and putting out fires. There will always be fires.

Nevertheless, don't underestimate the value of your presence and visibility to both your team and to management. You may not be the focus of activity any longer, but you need to understand what's happening with the project at all times. Issue Trackers and Defect Reports will continue to proliferate throughout development and testing (and beyond). You still need to be aware of them, you still need to be able to answer questions about them, and you still need to have a plan for resolving them. Nothing has changed about that.

Be Intentional About Transition Planning

The only way that you can work on a new Impossible Project is to be available. This means that you can't have an ongoing commitment to the project you just finished. As your Impossible Project approaches its conclusion you may start looking around for another project. Perhaps another Impossible Project. You may be recruited for one.

Make preparations to transition your responsibility at the end of the project. Be mindful of the transition and its impact to your team. Don't make a big deal about it. You're still in charge.

Nevertheless, as the centrality of your role diminishes, you will have the opportunity to give others more responsibility. Oftentimes this will be your partner. If not, work with management to identify your eventual replacement.

At some point, every Impossible Project must end. If it doesn't, then it has become, by definition, a Death March. Hopefully the project ends with some measure of success. Go back to the original vision and objectives to determine which were delivered and which fell short.

Your transition from the project should coincide with its completion, when the deliverables have been validated and everything is running smoothly. Don't leave early, and especially don't leave if residual issues remain. Run all the way through the finish line. You owe it to the project, to the team, and to yourself. You have earned the honor of leading the team in celebrating its accomplishments! And now is the time to celebrate. And rest. The team will be tired and need some time to recover and recuperate. You, will too.

In the movie *The Mission*, former mercenary Rodrigo Mendoza does penance by dragging a net carrying all of his possessions through a muddy mountain forest. When he receives forgiveness, the bundle is cut away and rolled over the cliff, his burden relieved and his life changed. He is free!!

You've successfully delivered your Impossible Project.

You've transitioned leadership.

And now you're ready to deliver your next Impossible Project.

A Pivotal Lesson

I'll conclude with a lesson that changed the trajectory of my career, and directly enabled my participation in all of the Impossible Projects that I subsequently pursued.

I had just delivered a core component of a major new system and I was very proud of it.

About a year later, my wife was pregnant with our first child. I knew that I wanted to take time off to be with them, so it was critical that someone besides me knew how to manage that component. As the second trimester progressed into the third, I started spending time with a co-worker, showing her how the component worked, how to run it, and how to monitor it.

We'd been working together for a couple of weeks when our manager met with a group that was interested in using the new system. This kind of meeting was routine. We'd done several before. But this one took a different turn.

When it came time to discuss how my component worked, our manager turned to my co-worker and asked her to explain it.

I was furious. After all, it was mine. I wrote it. I kept it running. I was the one who introduced it to other groups.

I sat there fuming for a minute, but then I started listening and realized that my co-worker was explaining it all exactly right. Everything. I went from angry to relieved to excited. I can vividly recall the abrupt reversal of emotion even now.

In that moment I had an epiphany: I was free to take time off without worrying about my component. She would have it covered. And she did. I didn't get a single call while

I was out. When I returned, I was free to pursue other challenges.

Since then, I've made a career out of getting projects off the ground, shepherding their delivery, then transitioning them to others. It can be hard to let go and you might spend some time adrift looking for the next project, but I've found that it is more than worth it. The Secrets shared in this book are the distillation of those experiences.

I will always be grateful to my co-worker and our manager for this pivotal lesson learned so early.

Bonus Secret: Revealed

Transition Leadership When the Project is Delivered

- The only way that you can work on a new Impossible Project is to be available.

- Give your partner and other team members more responsibility as the project nears completion.

- Stay visible and engaged all the way to the end of the project. Run through the finish line.

- Transition the last of your responsibility at the end of the project.

- Celebrate!! Then rest. Then start your next Impossible Project.

Acknowledgments

First and foremost, I am deeply grateful to those, too many to count, with whom I have had the honor of serving on Impossible Projects. The successes were a direct result of your efforts. This book is dedicated to those who had the greatest impact, and I apologize to anyone I have inadvertently omitted.

This book might not have happened without Stephen Brobst and John Ladley, who encouraged me to develop the idea and start writing. Sometimes it just takes a little nudge. Thanks also to friend and author Amy Lauren Miller for sharing her experience and advice.

I owe a huge debt of gratitude to Terrance Cooper, Lydia Schowalter, and Paul Schowalter who volunteered their time to edit and proofread. Their expertise, insights, and feedback significantly improved the content of this book from first draft to final publication. Any errors and omissions are my own.

Finally, the most special thanks to my wife Karen for her support and encouragement in pursuing this project and getting it out the door.

Meet the Author

Dr. Mark Cooper has more than thirty years of experience in enterprise architecture, and data and analytics. During that time he led and successfully delivered several Impossible Projects. His contributions and innovations have been recognized with the highest individual and corporate team awards, industry awards, and a US Patent. He has presented at conferences around the world, published six family history books, and founded a data-oriented consultancy. Mark earned a bachelor of science degree from Duke University, and a masters degree and doctorate from UCLA where his concentration was Artificial Intelligence. He and his family live near Memphis, Tennessee with their menagerie of dogs, cats, chickens, goats, and bees.

You can contact Dr. Cooper at:

https://www.linkedin.com/in/mark-g-cooper/

https://thedatabrains.com/

www.ingramcontent.com/pod-product-compliance
Lightning Source LLC
Chambersburg PA
CBHW040856210326
41597CB00029B/4867